HOW I GET
THROUGH LIFE

Also by Charles Grodin:

It Would Be So Nice If You Weren't Here

Charles Grodin

HOW I GET THROUGH LIFE

A Wise and Witty Guide

William Morrow and Company, Inc.
New York

It is the policy of William Morrow and Company, Inc., and its imprints and affiliates, recognizing the importance of preserving what has been written, to print the books we publish on acid-free paper, and we exert our best efforts to that end.

Library of Congress Cataloging-in-Publication Data

Grodin, Charles.
    How I get through life: a wise and witty guide / by Charles Grodin.
        p.   cm.
    ISBN 0-688-11258-7
    I. TITLE.
PN6162.G79   1992
814'.54—dc20   91-38238
                                                                    CIP

Printed in the United States of America

First Edition

1 2 3 4 5 6 7 8 9 10

BOOK DESIGN BY NICOLA MAZZELLA

To my wife,
Elissa

Acknowledgments

I would like to thank my editor, Lisa Drew, for her skill, sensitivity, and kindness.

Bob Shuman, Lisa's assistant, makes the tedious, technical side of writing a book actually pleasant, because I get to deal with him.

I'd like to thank my representative, Joy Harris, for her availability, energy, and optimism.

Lastly, I would like to thank all my friends and family for helping me get through life. The letters from all the people I don't know don't do me any harm either.

Contents

HOW I GET THROUGH LIFE

Preface

AFTER MY FIRST BOOK, which dealt with how to get through a life in show business, I spent a couple of years thinking about what I could write next. Not that there was this clamor for me to write another book. It's true my first book was successful. It even made some best seller list one week. Still, to be honest, there was no clamor. The closest thing to clamor might be from some of the letters I got from people who read my first book and found it helpful. Frankly those letters were the most gratifying response to anything I've ever done in my professional life. Still, to call it clamor, "a loud demand," would be an exaggeration at best.

No, this book that follows is really *my* idea and not the result of a loud demand. Since I love sitting in my Stratolounger writing things more than just about anything in life, I was determined to come up with an idea for another book. My only rule was that it have a higher aspiration than my first book. Somewhere I got the idea that your aspirations had to get higher as you went along. I'm not sure why. It's just an idea I heard that stuck. Since I didn't want to be ridiculed for *lower* aspirations right out of the box, I set out on the high road. Starting at the top, a rewrite of the Bible definitely seemed out of the question. Then one day I thought, "How about life itself—anything on that?" After all, get-

15

ting through life itself was the only thing I had any experience with that might be considered harder than
surviving in show business—maybe. As I mulled it over,
I remembered a line I had in a play once. The man apolo-
gizes to the woman for his poor behavior by saying, "I'm
sorry, Doris, but lately it just seems like it's one goddamned thing after another." The line invariably brought
tears to the audience's eyes, the woman's eyes, and my
eyes. That seems to be the one thing every person on
earth has in common. "Lately it just seems like it's one
goddamned thing after another."

I felt that long before I had the line in the play, and
first unconsciously, then consciously I began to develop
some plan, so life wouldn't often seem that way.

I formed a set of rules, certain procedures to get
around all this bad feeling, and it pretty much worked. I
was much happier. True, I was considered by many to
be incredibly controlling. There were so many things I
wouldn't do, so many places I wouldn't go. I have to
admit I even became an object of some ridicule. Good-
natured (to my face anyway), but still ridicule. The only
thing was that I seemed to be a lot happier than all the
people making fun of me. As years went by, some of my
ridiculers became a little more controlling themselves and
happier. They even admitted it.

So here's the second book. Basically I've covered a
lot of things that come up in life and what I do about
them. Some of these solutions may not work for you, but
I doubt they'll hurt.

There are no illegitimate children—only illegitimate parents.

—LEON R. YANKWICH

Parents

MOST OF THE PEOPLE I know hate their parents. My more loving friends hate only one parent and are indifferent toward the other. And they can tell you why. One mother told a daughter she was a failed abortion. The mother of a male friend with an early potty training problem put feces in his face as a way of hastening the process.

Mostly the reasons are more like "They never treated me as an individual"; "I only did what they wanted. I never learned what I wanted"; "They left me with sitters every chance they got." Normal everyday abuse.

I always loved my parents even though I, too, recall a fair amount of ridicule. I was constantly trying to call family meetings so we could all talk together. It wasn't silence at dinner, but it wasn't the Kennedys either. Mom and Dad would say, "Talk? All this kid wants to do is talk." No meetings were held. I loved my parents because I thought they did the best they could with the hands they were dealt. Dad was sickly and died young, and Mom shoveled the coal so our house would be warm. I noticed that I was able to hold on to a decent self-image even with the ridicule. On balance I gave them a break, and myself as well. I've saved a lot of energy not disliking my parents and a lot of therapy money, too.

We're imperfect people in an imperfect world, so I figure let's move on. Of course, nobody ever called me a failed abortion. If anyone had, I probably would have thought, "What a stupid jerk Mom or Dad is. I wonder how they got that way."

Or possibly, I'd be a hater, too.

[Key to longevity] Keep breathing.

—SOPHIE TUCKER

Staying Healthy

TO A CASUAL OBSERVER I might appear as someone who gets sick a lot, even though I virtually never get sick.

The reason for this discrepancy is that I have a high awareness of the subject. You might hear me discussing the temperature of a room far more than the average American. Words like "thermal underwear," "fans," "heaters," "humidifiers," "drafts," "vitamin C," "a lot of liquids," "aspirin" turn up in my conversation more than I'm happy to admit. But I am not a sick guy; I'm a preventive medicine guy.

I watch my weight. I'm not the thinnest person around—but not bad. I'll even lift a small barbell or two on occasion. I'm certainly not what you'd call a developed body guy—but OK.

Also, in spite of all the mystery surrounding the subject, I feel I know what causes the common cold. I have never in my life gotten a cold that I could not trace to being preceded by *being* too cold. This almost always has happened when I'm asleep since when I'm awake, I've got all the bases covered. For some reason it's taken me an extraordinarily long time to figure out that generally, it gets colder as the night goes on. So what feels like a nice cool, comfortable room to fall asleep in—around 4:00 A.M. can become an icebox.

I figure all I have to do now to prevent colds totally is to find a way to be alert when I'm asleep.

If you don't know where you are going, you will wind up somewhere else.

—Yogi Berra

Travel

I'M NOT A TRAVELER. I have to travel a lot in my line of work, so when I'm not working, I'm not going anywhere. In fact, there have been days at the end of which I could tell you how many times I've moved my body at all.

Personally I feel the whole subject is overrated. I'm basically a "look in your backyard" type of person. In my work I've gone to some pretty exotic places like Acapulco and New Zealand, for example. In Acapulco I saw guys dive off cliffs. In New Zealand I saw deer farms. I had seen both things on TV, and to tell you the truth, it wasn't that different being there. Also in Acapulco some locals murdered the bodyguard of the female star of the picture I was working on in order to steal a Cadillac. That really took the edge off Acapulco.

I know most people probably travel to "get away." The only thing I'm really interested in getting away from is myself, and of course, I was there in Acapulco and New Zealand.

I've worked in Guaymas, Mexico, which is known for its shrimp—period. Hawaii was breathtakingly beautiful, but when I arrived for work in the picture *King Kong*, I was informed the only way to get to and from work was by helicopter through high mountain ranges. I kind of got used to that around the time to leave. I

27

worked in Puerto Rico when I was in my twenties. Where I was, it was gorgeous. This one was definitely my fault. I thought I could get a deep tan by staying on the beach for six hours the first day. I wasn't hospitalized, but close. I worked in Morocco, which is close to Libya, at the height of our problems with Qaddafi. In Casablanca I went to a place they called Rick's Café, but without Bogart and Ingrid Bergman or the clientele from the movie, it just seemed like a Marriott cocktail lounge.

So all in all I prefer home—my bed, my chair, my language. I know I sound unbelievably provincial, but there're so many millions of people who love to travel *someone* has to stay home.

A friend may well be reckoned the masterpiece of Nature.

—RALPH WALDO EMERSON

Friendship

I'VE ALWAYS PUT AN unusually high premium on friendship. I remember as a boy darting away from the dinner table halfway through a meal because a pal had called and said he needed me for something. My mother would comment negatively, "This kid will do anything for his friends." It's not that my mother wasn't a great friend. It's just she wouldn't dart away from the dinner table unless it was pretty serious—and I'm sure when I darted, it wasn't.

I've always prided myself that when a friend asks me if I'll do him a favor, I say, "Sure," not "What?"

But as devoted as I am, I have stopped seeking out certain friends on more than one occasion.

One friend became overtly hostile, not just to me but to everyone. I chose not to confront this person. I just stopped calling. I think *that* was cowardly. I probably felt if I asked him why he was being so hostile, he would viciously turn on me in the middle of the inquiry.

I lost another friend because of the person's inability to stop talking. I did speak to this friend about it, but my friend couldn't stop talking long enough to really hear me. This friend lost a lot of friends.

I stopped seeking out another friend because *every* call was accompanied by a request for help of some kind—and not necessarily in times of need. This person came to believe it just wasn't worth talking to someone unless he could do something for you.

I've also avoided another person who made a concerted effort to become a friend. This person praised me to the skies. "You are the most intelligent, the most sensitive, the most generous," and then she'd ask for something. After hearing yourself described as Jesus Christ, how could you refuse? I did. I'm actually proud of not having that friend.

I've certainly had complaints about me from friends. One couple took me aside and told me I was telling too many stories. They weren't saying the stories weren't good or funny, just that so many of them stopped the natural flow of conversation. When I told someone of the complaint against me, she said, "There is no such thing as too many funny stories." But I cut way back. Actually I was so embarrassed by the comment I turned into a complete listener type, with that couple anyway. Eventually I started cutting back on stories everywhere for a time and have never really regained my former exuberance.

On balance, though, I still feel having good friends clearly is one of the necessities of getting through life. The boy somehow knew that when he darted away from the table.

As I grow older and older,
And totter towards the
   tomb,
I find that I care less and less
Who goes to bed with
   whom.

—DOROTHY L. SAYERS

Sex

I'VE HAD A LOT of trouble with sex in my life. It hasn't been the usual kinds of trouble—functioning, sexual identity, getting girls to have it with me, etc. My trouble has been in attitude.

When I grew up in the fifties in Pittsburgh, nobody had sex. I mean, nobody I knew of. Sex wasn't in the air very much at all. I remember as a boy of ten seeing some pornographic comic books that were floating around the schoolyard. That certainly got my attention, but actual sex in my life was nonexistent. Occasionally there'd be a murky distant whisper about some older girl in high school who may have, but it was all pretty removed.

The deal was clear. Nice girls didn't have sex until they were married, and everybody seemed to want to be in that category. That was it. It wasn't even a question.

Suddenly one day it was the sixties, and it was all different. Now a girl could have sex and still be nice. In fact, if you *didn't* have sex, you were weird. It was a whole new ball game. As far as I could see everyone, girls and certainly guys, was much happier. I was happier, too, until one day I met a girl I felt serious about, and it seemed we were moving toward sex. That's when I discovered I had a problem. I deeply felt, in spite of what society was saying, that if we had sex (she was a virgin), I would be obligated to propose marriage, and

35

just being out of my teens, I didn't really want to get married so fast. I had just come to New York, and this was the first girl I had gone out with. We didn't do it, and I went home for the summer. When I came back to New York in the fall, she told me she'd had sex with someone else. I was crushed.

I couldn't seem to make the transition everyone else made. The idea the girl had to be a virgin when you got married had been so strongly pounded into my consciousness it stuck. For years that became a major consideration for any woman I was seriously interested in. Was she a virgin? And if not—how many men? I definitely passed up some real serious possibilities, because the women had made the transition into modern times and I hadn't. And it wasn't the kind of thing you could come right out and hit a woman with. "By the way, are you a virgin? Oh, really? Well, how many men have you slept with?" One was too many.

Since I couldn't come out and ask the question, I had to do it more like Peter Falk as Columbo. "This fella you mentioned earlier that you went dancing with—how long did you know him? Two years? Uh-huh. And would you say he was a friend? More than a friend. A good friend? How good? Very good." My heart rapidly sinking, I tried to change the subject but couldn't. I was obsessed. "Now if you knew a fella for two years and he was a very good friend, and you were dancing with him and at the end of the evening you kissed good-night, and he wanted to come in . . ." Oh, it was a mess! Mostly because I almost always got answers that sent me out in search of the next possible virgin.

I went to therapists, talked to friends, people my age I went to school with, same background, everything. They didn't seem to have the problem. No one was that crazy about hearing of former lovers, but it wasn't a killer issue.

And then, one day out of the blue, almost as suddenly as the problem started, it went away.

I discovered death and became acutely aware of my own mortality. A series of events quickly happened, too morbid to recount, and suddenly I had a new obsession—death. Next to death, virginity and the number of partners anyone had had seemed barely of interest. I was on to bigger game, and the sex battle was over. Ironically, as the issue of mortality consumed me, I longed for my old body-count days.

I refused to attend his funeral, but I wrote a very nice letter explaining that I approved of it.

—MARK TWAIN

The D Word

I FIRST MET DEATH when my father died suddenly when I was eighteen, but it wasn't death that filled my thoughts for the next decade: It was my father. When I kind of emerged from under my black cloud, I walked into the sexual thing, which, as I've said, took over the trouble department pretty thoroughly. I'm sure they're all related, but right now life seems too short to figure that one out.

I tried to enjoy life, have fun during all of this, but "fun" wasn't my middle name. "Try" was.

Death came to say a big personal hello around the time I turned fifty. That corresponded with the age of my dad's passing and also with some unusually rough career setbacks. Throw in a couple of cancer scares to close people and two personal losses of very close loved ones, and it looked like death was here to stay. It was a constant close companion. How close? Well, once I slipped in the shower, and as I was falling, the only thing I could hold on to were my thoughts of death.

During this period I tried to act as though I were still my old self, except people noticed I had gotten strangely quiet, and the idea of anything more ambitious than staring off into space or eating a sandwich seemed beyond me. I still did everything I was supposed to, but it was like a shell game, and I was the shell.

41

I sought out various therapists. "This death thing," I'd say. "I mean, it's a real thing. What're we going to do about death?" One doctor said, "How do you know I don't feel exactly the way you do?" I said, "Do you?" He said, "It doesn't matter what I feel." I thought I was on some game show and left. I asked various friends for their thoughts on the subject, but just like sex, everyone seemed to be handling it better than I did. One guy said, "I don't know, everyone does it. I guess I can, too." Another male friend my age didn't respond at all but just made a downward pushing movement with his hands, indicating he chose not to relate to it. He then changed the subject and seemed to enjoy himself the rest of the evening while I sat there politely, still trapped in death's throes. One female friend referred to it as "the D word" and quickly changed the subject. Another just left the room like a shot. I seemed to be the only person I knew who had dived into this headlong. Just as I was about to give up on the therapy solution, one doctor said something that allowed me to see (if you'll pardon the expression) a tiny bit of light at the end of the tunnel. She said everyone past a certain age thought about death; it's just to what degree and what they thought that, of course, varied. Obvious but helpful.

So I set out to change my degree of thinking and what I thought. Thinking about death had basically become my full-time job. I figured my degree of available time to think about it would be lessened if I put myself on work overload, rather than underload, which thoughts of death had caused. I took on or created about six jobs for myself, and I plunged in no matter what I was thinking about. In my spare time I read every book related to life after death I could lay my hands on. After reading about thirty books, I had to decide whether I thought about a million people made up these stories or there was something to them.

Today I continue to be very busy, and any thought of death is immediately joined by thoughts of life after death, and that life always retains everything good in this life and then some. Call me crazy—it works.

Also, I have a four-year-old son. Nicky demands that I think about life more fully than I ever have before. How I deal with death turned out really to be about diving more into life. I highly recommend it as a solution should you ever run into the above.

Angels can fly, because they take themselves lightly.

—G. K. Chesterton

People Who Talk About Themselves

SPARE ME FROM PEOPLE who tell you everything that's happened to them since you've last seen them—without a moment's interest in you.

Let's assume that these are needy people, but who isn't? Those of us who are polite and could pass as good listeners can pay a mean price.

NEEDY PERSON

God, it's so good to see you. I have so much to tell you!

POLITE LISTENER
(famous last words)

How are you?

Much later, after they've exhausted themselves talking about themselves, they have to go—presumably to find someone else who hasn't heard their story.

Any attempt on the listener's part to share something from his life is received by the needy person with a glazed look, as though he's going through a flashing yellow light at an intersection—a momentary pause in his journey of self-expression.

47

If these needy people understood that they make their listener feel depressed and then invisible, maybe they'd stuff it.

As for me, I've developed a glazed look myself that eventually slows the talkers/takers down. It doesn't stop them, but it slows them down. It's a beginning.

Life is too short to stuff a mushroom.

—Shirley Conran

Restaurants

I HAVE ANNOYED PEOPLE because of my choice of restaurants. Or maybe I should say lack of choice. I have no spirit of adventure on the subject. If I find a restaurant I like, that's where I go—period. I have no interest whatsoever in checking out "the wonderful new Polynesian place that just opened." I've never been to the old one.

It's not new things I'm interested in; it's old things. I like the old familiar dishes, but mostly I like the old familiar waiters. In New York I have been to the same place so regularly that when I come in, you'd think I was the owner. I mean, they don't lift me on their shoulders—but close. In a new place they most likely will say, "We can only seat you at five or nine-thirty, Mr. Gordon."

In Los Angeles in the sixties I went to a place called the La Brea Inn for prime rib and afterward to an ice-cream parlor called Will Wright's for hot fudge sundaes. Over a period of months I went to the La Brea Inn, then Will Wright's; the La Brea Inn, then Will Wright's; the La Brea Inn, then Will Wright's. The woman I was with started taking tranquilizers.

I particularly liked Japanese restaurants for a while, until the waiters' upset over my ordering sixteen pieces of the same type of sushi made it impossible for me to return.

51

At one time I used to frequent an Italian restaurant that I referred to as "right next door to one of the finest Italian restaurants in the city." I didn't go to the *really* good place because not only did you need a jacket and tie, you got the feeling you had to sit at attention, too.

The biggest problem I have with restaurants is when some friends forcibly wedge me out of my pattern to try some fancy new place. Here I have to listen to the "specials." Peter Falk, a most concentrated fellow, told me he has never had to concentrate so hard as he does on the recitation of specials. Unlike Peter, after the first ten I can no longer bring myself to listen. Mostly my thoughts are, "How long is this going to go on? Is anyone else getting dizzy?" After about fifteen (it may only be eight), I start thinking about how funny a scene this could be in a movie—where a perfectly normal-looking diner, after hearing ten specials, suddenly starts to scream and turns the table over. Truthfully, somewhere early on, all I really hear are smidgens: "That's diced, not sliced"; "They sprinkle bayberry herb over the . . ." "and it comes with a lemon vinaigrette sauce that they . . ." Toward the end of the list I admit my thoughts are of a more hostile nature. "I'm going to eat it, not frame it." I'm really put to the test when after the completion, the enthusiastic reciter asks, "Any questions?" Recently this was done by a short, heavyset chef with a chimneylike hat. My question was, "Do you keep anything under your hat?" There was an awkward silence. I quickly jumped in with an apologetic "I bet you get asked that a lot." He shot me a thin smile and said, "Not really."

All in all, on those special occasions, I think everyone would be a lot happier if I stayed home.

If you can't say anything good about someone, sit right here by me.

—ALICE ROOSEVELT LONGWORTH

Gossip

I DON'T LIKE GOSSIP—never have. As a teenager I remember driving around with a group of pals as each recounted what he was able to "get" off his date of the night before. I sat quietly and listened to how one guy felt a breast, another danced with his body pressed close, etc. When my turn came, I angered everyone by refusing to participate. "You listened to what we said," they charged. I asked, "What should I have done, thrown myself out of the car?"

Gossip chills my soul. It reduces people's lives to idle banter.

Today when it comes up—and it's always presented gleefully like the high point of the evening—I either stare blankly or change the subject. I figure that's better than embarrassing everyone by saying, "This is not for me." Better, but not much.

People find it hard to believe I don't like gossip. I don't dislike it as much as dirty jokes, which people also can't believe I don't like. I try not to think much about what kind of impression I make in life, but I do at those dirty joke moments. I wonder where anyone got the impression I'd like to know what the penis said to the vagina. Maybe people think all men like that stuff.

I guess what bothers me most about gossip is it always gives me the feeling that no one cares about anyone else. That's just one of the reasons I've stayed so close to my mother over the years. My mother wells up with tears easily over the misfortune of strangers. Come to think of it, I've *never* heard her gossip. Maybe if I had been a gossip columnist's son, I'd love it.

We have just enough religion to make us hate, but not enough to make us love one another.

—JONATHAN SWIFT

Religion

I NEVER REALLY UNDERSTOOD religion. My mother kept a kosher home. We had different sets of dishes and silverware for meat and dairy, and another set for Passover. If a fork from the dairy set or a spoon from Passover, for example, somehow got anywhere else (highly unlikely), it was thrown away. I never understood it. I'm sure it was explained to me more than a couple of times, but I don't remember the explanation.

My father wasn't religious. He was mad at the synagogue for something that happened when he lost his father. Nobody ever told me what happened, and I chose not to ask.

I went to Hebrew school for about six years. I had a wonderful rabbi—Rabbi Kaplan. He told colorful stories from the Old Testament. I learned to read Hebrew, but I didn't know what anything meant.

As years went by, my mother would regularly chastise me with lines like "I bet you don't even know next week is Rosh Hashana." I didn't. As a boy I would fast on Yom Kippur the way you're supposed to, but then I stopped doing that.

Once I went into an empty church just to check out what it looked like, and someone chased me out.

I guess I should feel bad about my ignorance of the different religions and their customs, but I don't.

I put all my fervor in that department not on religion but ethics. I'm big on ethics. Ethics is my religion.

I respect all religions and understand none.

I was much too far out all my life,
And not waving, but drowning.

—STEVIE SMITH

Therapy

SOME OF THE SMARTEST people I know are psychologically retarded because of a closed attitude toward therapy. I think it should be a required course starting in grammar school. I believe it would be helpful for people to be able to talk about what they feel and try to understand why. I rate it a little more important than spelling.

Here are some things I've learned over the years in therapy. I believe some people might know all this without any guidance, but I doubt that it's more than a small minority.

1. If you're a man who hooks up with a woman who doesn't like her father, look out.
2. If you're a woman who hooks up with a man who doesn't like his mother, it can be even worse.
3. If you hook up with someone who hates either parent, watch out.

(I'm not saying the above will always be true; just keep your eyes open.)

4. Most people are much more on edge than you think they are. I think it's a good idea to treat people generally as though they're just coming off

drugs—carefully, gently. The worse that will happen is that people will think you're unusually sensitive.

5. If you're having trouble in your main relationship, and you notice you have trouble in other relationships and your partner doesn't, it's probably you.
6. Don't speak up every time something bothers you. You'll be speaking up all over the place. Pick your spots.
7. Nice doesn't mean weak any more than not nice means strong. It's usually the other way around.
8. "Do unto others as you would have them do unto you" really is a great idea. They don't call it the Golden Rule for nothing.
9. I try to avoid judging. "Let him who is without sin cast the first stone." That's my personal favorite.

A lot of the above can be found in the Bible, but I've felt a certain superior attitude can attach itself to people who only get the goods there. I'm sure people who get their insights from therapy can feel superior, too. So my last one would be:

10. Don't ever think you're smarter or better than anyone. You'd be amazed how wrong you might be.

All the modern inconveniences.

—MARK TWAIN

Modern Times

THE OTHER DAY WHEN a commercial came on, I automatically pressed "Muting" on the TV remote control and realized what a great modern development muting is.

Essentially I've remained a 1950s guy, but I do recognize a good invention when I see it. "Seek and Scan" on my car radio you can have. I have never mastered seek and scan. I just don't know what they're for. I thought it was perfect when you had your on/off knob and a tuner to find the station. Period. That's it. Fine. Now you can seek or scan and lock in stations. What?

I know computers are great. I'm sure they are. Some really smart people have told me, but when I would try to rent a car and the computer was inevitably "down," I wondered. Even when it wasn't down, it seemed to take longer than just filling out the form with a pen. In any case, I certainly don't feel in a position to question computers since I'm a man who doesn't own a typewriter.

For most of my adult life I never even had a stove.

I lived in an apartment hotel on the Upper West Side in Manhattan. I moved in in 1967, when I had no money, and just stayed there until well after I was playing leading roles in movies. I had a living room, a bedroom, and a kitchenette. This was a building largely inhabited by low-income or no-income elderly people and by poor students. Once after it was announced in the papers that I was about to fly to London to play opposite Candice Bergen in a movie, an elderly woman on the elevator looked at me quizzically and asked, "Do they pay you right in these movies?" A friend came to visit and remarked that my place looked like the apartment of someone who once met a celebrity. Another visitor said, "I know a good lawyer who could get you out of here." It was rare, though, that anyone visited the place until around 1980, when I had a pinched nerve and was laid up for a while. A female friend came over to cook dinner. I was lying on the sofa in the living room. I watched her as she went into the tiny kitchenette and fully turn around twice before saying, "You have no stove." I sincerely asked, "What's a stove?" meaning, What does a stove do that my little broilerette and double burner (two hot plates) couldn't do? The answer was "Nothing." What others saw as strange deprivation, I didn't. I saw a view of the river and the sky from both rooms, also from the inside of the shower. It was as close to quiet as you could get in New York. I was on the twenty-second floor. *I* saw a great apartment. I can only remember once covering for the place. A world-famous actress called me and said, "Charles, the switchboard put me right through. They're not screening your calls!" I said indignantly, "I'll have to speak to them about that!" I don't live there now because I got married and my wife didn't quite see it as I did.

Back to the subject of muting, I once had a great idea. If you're in a phone conversation you wish you weren't in, hang up—but do it while *you're* talking, then leave the phone off the hook and say, "I tried to call you back and just got a busy signal." I've never done this, but I believe it could work nicely.

[On his wife's observing him kissing a chorus girl] I wasn't kissing her, I was whispering into her mouth.

—CHICO MARX

Jealousy

ALTHOUGH I NEVER WANTED to admit it to myself, I think I was insecure regarding women for the first thirty or so years of my life. Aside from my upbringing that said every woman had to be a virgin at marriage, the unusual degree of my interest in a woman's romantic past had to be that of an insecure person. Over the years, as I've said, I've grown out of that preoccupation and been able to, if you'll pardon the expression, put it to bed.

Today I consider myself average normal on the subject, which means it's still not my favorite subject—more like it's *not* a subject. Oh, like any average normal guy, if anyone comes on to my wife at a party, I'll notice it, but that's never really happened except in the case of the late . . . I'd rather not mention his name because no one knows it was me who killed him.

The subject of jealousy comes up in my life today not personally but professionally. For some reason I can't explain but am deeply grateful for, as much as I had the problem personally, that's as little as I've had it professionally. Mostly I've had it when I see political operatives in show business with less talent than others do extraordinarily well. I'm talking about people who think about PR more than they think about their work. People who give and go to a lot of parties. I know one guy who had two studio heads as godfathers of his children.

73

For the most part, overwhelmingly, I understand the careers of successful people in show business. Whether I'm a particular fan or not, I can see why someone is successful. The opposite end of the spectrum was Al Jolson. I once had an agent, an older man, who represented Jolson when the agent was starting. He told me at the height of Jolson's success he could become startlingly agitated if a juggler in Toledo got a rave review in *Variety*. "What the hell could a juggler do to get a rave like that?" he reported Jolson raging.

Then there's the comedian who returned from a successful tour telling a comic friend, "I killed them in Boston. I murdered them in Philly. They loved me in Detroit. I didn't do so great in St. Louis. They were screaming in Seattle, Denver, and Los Angeles." The other comedian asks, "So what happened in St. Louis?"

It always seems that comedians, actors, and actresses are most critical of other comedians, actors, and actresses. No one seems to notice what they're saying about themselves when they are beating up on someone whose job they can do.

It's sad to say, but people seem to mind the success of strangers less than the success of friends. People can handle friends' failures quite comfortably.

Obviously there's always more than one successful person in a profession, and we should know that our lives are made richer by others' good work. I only wish I could have felt the same about my girl friends' former lovers.

When a man is wrapped up in himself he makes a pretty small package.

—JOHN RUSKIN

Missing the Obvious

IT TOOK ME YEARS to understand that if you were consistently unhappy in a relationship, it was probably not a good relationship.

I know people who actually didn't realize that if they don't eat, they'll feel weak. These are people with degrees.

There are many people walking around shivering in freezing climates who never heard of thermal underwear.

People who promise you that if elected, they'll work twenty-four hours a day don't seem to know how dangerous that is. Administrators at hospitals have people working twice that long. That's a plan they must have made when they didn't have enough sleep.

People who yell at people don't seem to know they'll be hated, usually forever.

People who whack their children around don't seem to know that most of the prison population were whacked around as kids.

When you go to war, you don't "kick butt"; you kill people and get killed.

People who ignore severe medical symptoms because they don't believe in doctors usually die.

If you spend more time being aware of how the other person feels, you'll have a more successful life.

Don't tell anyone how wonderfully you're doing unless it's your mother.

Older people, not in wonderful health, shouldn't do things as though they were thirty. I've lost two older friends because that wasn't obvious to them.

A verbal contract isn't worth the paper it's printed on.

—SAMUEL GOLDWYN

Lawsuits

I'VE ONLY BEEN INVOLVED in one lawsuit in my life. I was supposed to do a movie with Jill Clayburgh in the late seventies, and at the last minute Jill decided not to do it. I had been working on the script and interviewing directors with the writer and producer for several weeks. I had put in a great deal of time, and one day I heard the whole thing was off. Nobody phoned me. They just walked away.

I had a contract—not a signed contract. Most of my movie contracts have never been signed. There were a few open points that hadn't been agreed on. This is generally true of these unsigned contracts. For example, for a long time I never wanted to sign a contract that committed me to tour the country to publicize a movie I hadn't even made yet. Then one day my attorney said, "No movie company is going to ask you to talk to the press about a picture you end up not liking." These contracts seem like they're about a thousand pages long, so there's always stuff the attorneys never agree on. Since we agree on how much I'm paid and how long I have to work, I go to work without a signed contract. There's never been a problem, but on the other hand, I never worked for a long time with people in preproduction who walked away from the movie either. If they had called and told me something, anything almost, I wouldn't have sued. I never have before or since about anything, but I didn't like their walking away after all that work, so I had this lawsuit.

Generally the stress and expense of a lawsuit are not worth it, and besides, if I can possibly see the other guy's point of view, which I usually can, I'll let it go and chalk it up in the life-is-too-short department. Here I never even heard the other point of view. I just heard the sound of walking away.

Some people I know sent me to see some lawyers at this big firm Loeb & Loeb. I met with a sweet, easygoing, heavyset guy named Al Smith and a nice young woman named Sandy Froman. I told Al and Sandy that I had nothing to hide. I told them about all the work I had done and the walking-away thing. After looking at the small unresolved details of the unsigned contract, they felt, given industry practices, I had a good case.

Weeks went by. During that period the people I was suing sued me. I forget for what. Al and Sandy explained people often do that to scare you away. It didn't.

However, the day before the other side was to take my deposition, Al and Sandy called me into their offices and did scare me a little. They said that the other side was represented by a fairly legendary guy named Marshall Grossman, and that was not good news. "Why?" I asked cautiously. Grossman was an aggressive litigator, they explained, a hard-hitting, no-holds-barred type of guy. I blinked once and said, "But I have nothing to hide. Why should I worry?" They said they didn't want me to worry, but they just wanted to let me know that even if I had nothing to hide, this was going to be no picnic.

I left their offices somewhat preoccupied. At first it seemed to me the only thing I had to fear was fear itself, which, of course, isn't a lot of fun either.

I spent a sleepless night tossing and turning over what Marshall Grossman could nail me with. It really couldn't be points on the actual case, and yet a no-holds-barred guy might try anything. I felt before I could relax enough to fall asleep, I had to figure out just what it was I had to be afraid of, aside from fear.

Around 4:00 A.M. it hit me. Grossman could ask me how much I got paid. I'd tell him. Then he could dig out some awful review someone wrote about me somewhere at some time that I hadn't seen (because I don't seek those out), read it aloud, and then ask smugly, sarcastically, "And they're paying *you* how much?" etc., etc. I realized Al or Sandy might jump up mid-review and object, but Grossman might get out a couple of "lousy"s before they could object, and I'd have a "lousy" burned into my brain forever. I mean I've done really well in the review department, but a couple have slipped through and burned their way in there. There was a movie I wrote and starred in where someone said (and I don't have to look this up), "If you want to know what it feels like to die sitting upright in a theater seat, go see this movie." So that was my fear: Grossman burning a pan in on me.

The next day at the law offices I was anxious to see the legendary one. In he marched, and he was a little more than I imagined: six feet, muscular, dark hair, strong, thick mustache, short-sleeved brown shirt. He glanced over at me as he entered with a look you give a dish you're passing on the way to what you want on a smorgasbord.

There were about ten people in the room, from my side and the other side, with Grossman sitting opposite me. His first question was, "What is the extent of your education?" I said I was valedictorian of my high school class and—. He snapped, "I didn't ask you what honors you received!" For the next hour basically what he tried to do was discredit me. Whenever he opened his folder, I leaned over to see if there were any reviews in there but spotted nothing of a newspaper nature.

He was tough, but sometimes I wondered about the legendary status. Knowing that I claimed I worked on the script for several weeks, he asked if I was in the Writers Guild. A legendary guy should have known I was, but he asked the question. I said I was. Without missing a beat he asked, "Under what circumstances did you join?" I guess he hoped and even assumed it would be for some remote C movie situation. When I said I was hired by 20th Century-Fox to write the screenplay for Woody Allen's Broadway show *Play It Again, Sam,* he quickly said, "Strike the question." During a break early on, Al and Sandy told me that most of what he said they could object to, but since I seemed to be holding my own, they weren't objecting to anything.

Grossman could have asked if they used the script when they made the movie. They didn't, but the reasons for that turn out not too bad for me either. So far he hadn't really laid a glove on me. To tell the truth, I was kind of enjoying the whole thing, and strange as it may seem, so was he.

Then the questioning took a really weird turn. It seemed as though he was somehow trying to connect me to Jill Clayburgh's dropping out of the movie. Since that was the event that ostensibly caused the cancellation, and it had never really been explained, it seemed an OK direction to explore it except I knew she had been persuaded by some advisers that the script wasn't really good enough, and that was the reason she dropped out.

He began. "Have you ever visited Jill Clayburgh?" The question instantly suggested to me where he was going. Since I knew there was nothing there, I couldn't resist acting a bit uneasy before I admitted, "Yes."

"Where?" he quickly asked. "At her home," I uncomfortably acknowledged. "Was anyone else present?" "Yes." "Who?" "Her husband." He stared at me. "Have you ever been alone with her anywhere?" "Yes," I quickly said. "Where?" he asked. "In a restaurant for dinner," I announced, now really enjoying myself. He then spent the next five minutes trying to turn a family fish house into a dark place where couples have sex at their tables.

When the whole thing was over, Grossman shook my hand and allowed how he had enjoyed my work in the movies. I said I enjoyed his work as well.

The other side eventually settled the claim for about 25 percent of my salary, most of which went to legal fees. I felt pretty good about the whole thing. It was an interesting education.

The only downside I can think of is that I've now revealed a weakness. I can envision a scenario in the future where I have to sue over something (rats in an expensive rented house, for example, which I've almost but haven't done twice), and some attorney will whip out a lousy notice.

The life of a sailor is very unhealthy.

—Francis Galton

The Day I Won a Boat

ONE DAY I GOT a phone call from an excited associate of mine telling me I had just won a boat. The fellow giving me the good news was a very bright guy who was involved with me in producing a movie. The call had come into the production office, and everyone there was pretty excited about it. I immediately told my colleague I didn't believe it, that people were calling people all the time, especially in L.A., congratulating them on winning something—money, a boat, whatever. My associate said he was, of course, aware of this, but this boat guy was the real thing. He had been checked out, and he wouldn't have called me all excited if he and the others in the office weren't convinced I had actually won a boat. All I had to do to get my boat, and it wasn't a little one, by the way, was call this 800 number in the Midwest, answer some questions, and I'd soon be a boat owner. Just for the hell of it I took the number and said I would call the guy just to see how his scam worked. I thought it was totally irrelevant to mention to my associate that I had absolutely no interest in owning a boat. I always liked the saying "The two biggest days in a man's life are the day he buys a boat and the day he sells it."

I called the 800 number. The conversation went something like this:

BOAT GUY

Hello.

ME

Hello. My name is Charles Grodin. I just got a call from my office telling me I've won a boat and to call this number.

(A long pause)

BOAT GUY

Congratulations!

ME

Thank you. I'm a little surprised because I didn't enter any contest or anything. What kind of a boat is it?

BOAT GUY

It's a thirty-four-footer. Do you presently own a boat?

ME

No, I don't.

BOAT GUY

Do you enjoy boating?

ME

Not really. Will it cost me anything to get my boat?

BOAT GUY

Do you have friends who enjoy boating?

ME

Yes. How much will it cost me to get the boat?

BOAT GUY

Do you think owning a boat is something you could come to enjoy?

ME

No. What's this going to cost?

BOAT GUY

May I tell you all about the boat?

ME
How much will getting this boat cost?

The boat guy hung up on me.

This all happened about five years ago. I would love to think now I'm five years wiser, but a few months ago I got an envelope in the mail, and on the *outside* of the envelope it said, "Congratulations, Charles Grodin. You have won $100,000," and I opened the damn envelope just to make sure I hadn't.

Today one of my goals in life is to be able to immediately hang up the phone whenever anyone starts a conversation with the word "congratulations."

Of all the animals, the boy is the most unmanageable.

—PLATO

Children

AT THE BEGINNING OF *Godfather III* a voice-over says something like "Children are our only treasure. Not great sums of money, but children." I don't know who the voice belonged to, but I doubt it came from any of the main characters because they all conduct themselves so that most of their children are murdered, sometimes by each other.

It's amazing how different people's attitudes toward children are—even their own. I had one child when I was in my twenties, and another in my fifties. Most guys in their twenties who are wondering where the rent was coming from, which I was, don't spend a lot of time thinking about their children. Oh, I always adored my daughter—no question. It's just a matter of focus. I was so out of it, so stupid, so selfish that our activities together had to work for both of us—like watching a parade together or going to certain movies together, not movies she *alone* might like. I'm ashamed to admit I wasn't big on getting down on the floor and doing doll stuff either.

My best defense is I can't remember my parents ever doing anything of a playmate nature with me. *No* movies together—even ones *they* might like. My parents had no time left after running a store, making deliveries, cooking dinner, doing the washing, the ironing, the house-cleaning, etc. That's my defense. I never learned to play with children from my parents.

On the other hand, I've been friends a long time with a couple, where the husband, who I'm sure didn't have parents who played with him either, is always down on that floor with his kids.

My four-year-old son just knocked and then opened the door of my study and announced in his inimitable sound, "Your dinner's ready." I stared at him, falling deeper in love. He mistook the stare for noncomprehension, so he repeated his announcement. I said, "Thank you." He nodded and left. I'm better at this stuff now. I still have a lot on my mind, but I don't think about paying the rent. That's a big difference.

The biggest thing I learned about children over the years has to do with the issue of children's rights—a concept I was never even aware of until a few years ago.

Over the years this couple who are friends of mine treated their kids as equals, as adults. The thought of children having equal rights was planted in me watching my friends.

As a child I argued with my father for about four years over whether I should have to go to work in his store after school. I argued that I started kindergarten at four and at seven started Hebrew school for six years after regular school. After I was bar mitzvahed at thirteen, my father wanted me to come work in the store after school. I wanted to play ball. Sometimes he won. Sometimes I won—with a terrible penalty. I never really won my father's friendship. Even though I argued my case, actually wrote my case fervently (my father would only communicate through letters after a while, even though we lived in a small six-room house together), I never really thought I was right. It was only after this children's rights concept came to me that I realized I'd had some truth on my side—particularly since my father could easily have afforded to pay someone to do my job, which he eventually did.

So what are the rules? It suddenly seems simple. The kids are entitled to the same consideration and respect we give each other as adults—no more, no less.

Today my grown daughter hears from me probably more than anyone can use. There is some guilt there, but guilt aside, I'm her biggest admirer. She's actually one of my idols. In spite of all my stupid youthful parenting, I probably did something right, but mostly I think I got lucky. She, on the other hand, happily seems to like me more than she used to, or maybe it would be more accurate to say stuff about me that bothered her doesn't anymore. For example, she could never understand how I could speak about having done a good job on something. She thought that sounded too much like bragging. I explained that life and particularly my profession, show business, beat you down so much it was necessary to speak aloud at least to family when you felt you did well. After a few years in show business she now agrees with that one.

I also always felt that she sometimes struck up friendships with people before she really knew who they were. She thought I lived life too carefully. After a couple of surprises from "friends," she's leaning a little more in my direction on that one. For my part, I think she's loosened me up a little—not a lot, a little. In any case, as I've said, I'm crazy about her. Kind of makes you believe no matter what you did wrong, it's never too late.

Anybody can become angry—that is easy; but to be angry with the right person, and to the right degree, and at the right time, and for the right purpose . . . that is not within everybody's power and is not easy.

—ARISTOTLE

Perfectionists

I RECENTLY SPOKE TO an actress who had just finished working with one of our most celebrated film directors. I asked what he was like to work with. "He was a tyrant," she answered; "he screamed and yelled at everyone." Months later I saw the man interviewed on television. The reporter asked him what he was like to work with. "I'm murder on the set," he replied with a smile. In a most charming manner he went on to explain that he was a perfectionist. "I will sometimes ask someone to do something thirty times until I get exactly what I want." He grinned.

I have no problem with the thirty times deal. I can offhand think of two directors I've worked with (even more celebrated than this perfectionist) who might ask you to do something a lot more than thirty times. They would, I guess, consider themselves perfectionists as well, but they weren't screamers. They were soft-spoken gentlemen.

Of course, a desire for perfection is admirable, I guess, but certainly not when it's used as a rationale for abuse.

When people speak of themselves as perfectionists, what do they mean anyway? After all, it's not that easy to get anyone to agree on what's perfect. I think what they really mean is the second part of the director's answer: "to get exactly what I want." They throw the word "perfectionist" around; because it has such an admirable connotation, they hope it takes the onus off the screaming.

I once worked with a director who announced before we began that he was a screamer. He didn't bother calling himself a perfectionist. (He certainly lacked pretension, I'll give him that.) He didn't even claim he was going to scream to get exactly what he wanted. He just said he was going to scream. His only excuse was "It doesn't really mean anything." Apparently all the people he screamed at didn't agree, and after about a month he was fired. It was a very long month.

So who are all the screamers anyway? Of course, this question is not confined to show business but sadly applies to every business. Whether they call themselves perfectionists or not, they are insecure, desperate people.

The day that they put the treatment of others above their "perfectionism," is the day the drug and alcohol abuse rate will drop—at least a little around them.

"It's broccoli, dear."
"I say it's spinach, and I say the hell with it."

—E. B. WHITE

Diet

I'VE ALWAYS BEEN AMAZED at the amount of money people spend in order to find ways to lose weight.

Obviously the only way to lose weight is to eat less things that make you gain weight. Just as obviously for those millions of us who love pizza, cheeseburgers, etc., this is almost impossible to do. Some diets suggest eating more lettuce or drinking powdered things. I'm sure this works for a while, but who wants to go through life eating lettuce and drinking powder? Real good fattening food always seemed to me one of the things we had going for us in the happiness department.

Here's my solution, and it really works. It's not a book. It's not a pamphlet. It's not even one sheet of paper.

Drink water. Drink two full glasses of water before you set out to eat anything, and you'll lose weight. It really works. You just have to do it. If you want to be on a magazine cover or something, drink three glasses of water. Personally, even being in show business, I don't worry about the magazine cover, and I don't think you should either, so I stay with the two glasses. Let's forget about gorgeous and just try to avoid fat.

If you are distressed by anything external, the pain is not due to the thing itself, but to your own estimate of it. And this you have the power to revoke at any moment.

—MARCUS AURELIUS

Recovering from Being Left

I SAW A SITCOM on television recently about a pretty girl who left a nice-looking young guy "because the chemistry wasn't really there."

I'm sure being left by someone ranks right up there behind death and probably close to or slightly ahead of being fired. So this being left situation is definitely something to contend with.

On the sitcom the young guy was eventually pacified by his mother and friends by being told, "Everyone gets left at one time or another, and some people get left a lot." The show seemed to want to have a happy ending. I thought it was a very depressing treatment of the subject because it left out the main survival element of being left. Blame the other person! Oh, I believe we all have to look long and hard at ourselves in these situations, but we're usually so hurt that it's asking a lot to double up on the pain—so really blame that other person! Later it's probably a good idea to look at the full truth and your responsibility, but for now go after that leaver! In most cases you can really do a job on them, too. Number one, if you're so bad, what the hell kind of judgment did they have being with you in the first place!? Second, they've never made a relationship work in their life either! Just dwell on all their lousy stuff. You're so hurt it should come pretty easily to you.

One caution: Don't think they're sharp just because they were smart enough to leave you. That's a big temptation for anyone to think when they're down. At least for that first month stay on the offensive. Blame the other person!

And what have kings that privates
    have not too,
Save ceremony, save general ceremony?

—WILLIAM SHAKESPEARE

Kings and Queens and Things

A FRIEND OF MINE was in a movie that was financed by an English film company. It had a world premiere screening in New York, and he asked me to come. Afterward there was a reception given at a place called the British Film Institute.

Present at this event was a duchess of some kind who was a close relative of the queen of England. The duchess and her little group stood in an area elevated by three steps at the end of the room. No throne type of thing, but a little platform.

I've never really understood the whole royalty deal, but I know some people who have kings and queens and things get a little touchy if you question it, so I'll try to tread lightly here. I guess my big problem with it is, how did these people get to be kings in the first place? My limited research tells me that somewhere way back when, they headed up some groups that won a war or two, or if no war, they figured out a way to make a lot of money.

I'm afraid I've always been a little wary of people who make a lot of money from ways other than getting up and going to work. A guy who can make as much money in one phone call as another guy could in a lifetime of labor somehow makes me nervous. I'm not say-

113

ing I'm making sense; I'm just telling you how I feel. Anyway, royalty never did a lot for me. Mostly I watch in wonder at other people bowing.

This British Film Institute reception was, and is at this writing, the only time I've been in the presence of royalty. The royal party stayed gathered at their three-step-up place, and I stayed gathered down below with all the regular people.

The movie had a lot of weird sex and violence, not the kind of stuff you can chitchat about too easily at a British Film Institute gathering, so the conversation wasn't exactly flowing. As I wandered around the large room, I noticed that the duchess and her party stood, if not with their backs to the room, certainly not perusing it. Suddenly a man tapped me on the shoulder and asked me if I would like to meet the duchess. I didn't know who he was, but reflexively I just said, "Yes." He quickly took me by the arm and led me across the room and up the three steps to the royal party. He approached a small group and spoke to one of the men. "This is Charles Grodin," he said. "I think it would be so nice if he were to meet the duchess." The man he spoke to glanced at me for a fraction of a second, then turned back to his group. My guy said once more, a little louder: "This is Charles Grodin. He's a big American film star, and I think it would be so nice if he were to meet the duchess." The guy turns again and this time gives me a full second's look before he turns back to his group. I don't know who my guy was or who he worked for, but once again he repeated, in a voice a little more insistent: "It would be so nice if Mr. Grodin were to meet the duchess. He's a very big American film star!"

The duchess's guy now turned and stared at me. You could see he not only never heard of me but clearly didn't recognize me for a second either. I would have been embarrassed, but I was starting to get some weird enjoyment out of the whole scene. The English protector of the duchess seemed to be squirming with one of his major life decisions. Finally he took my arm away from the other man who had it and, with the tiniest of sighs, led me over to the duchess. "This is Charles Grodin. He's a major American film star," he said, without much enthusiasm, then turned abruptly and walked away, leaving me alone with the duchess.

The duchess appeared to be a woman in her late thirties with a pleasant expression on her face. We looked at each other for a moment as I tried to think of something to say. It seemed really out of line to mention the weird movie, so I said what a nice room we were standing in. She agreed. I was pretty much out of topics right there. I decided to just be myself and hope I wouldn't offend. "I've never met any royalty," I said. "I don't really know anything about it. What's the main focus of your life?"

She looked dumbfounded, then quickly recovered her composure. There's no question I had inadvertently caught her with a low blow right off the bat. Trying to buy time, I'm sure, she said, "I don't understand your question."

I said again, trying to speak in a more delicate tone, "What do you mostly do or think about or, uh, focus on?"

She continued to stare at me uncomfortably. After what seemed an interminable pause, she said, "My family." I waited, but that's all she would say. We stood there a moment longer trying to look pleasantly at each other. Then she said: "I wouldn't normally ask you such a question, but since you asked me, what is *your* main focus in life?"

I said my main focus was talking to people kind of

like we're doing now. She smiled uncomfortably at me and clearly communicated that my life must be a living hell with all this people-to-people talking.

I liked her. I didn't really understand why the whole encounter was so uncomfortable, but I liked the way she was trying to hang in there. For all she knew, I could have asked her who was *in* her family, possibly causing an international incident, but I refrained. Since the silence seemed to be now coming in waves, I said it was very nice to have met her and left.

The duchess's guy scrutinized me carefully as I headed down the three steps. Seeing that the crown was still safe and the royal family hadn't fallen, he turned back to his group.

Later on in the evening I found myself chatting with a vivacious Englishwoman who seemed to be a part of the royal group but a regular person. I told her of my encounter, mostly with the guy who had been trying to protect the duchess. She chuckled and said, "They go a bit overboard sometimes." After some more chatting, it came out that I would be going to London in a few months for a movie. She gave me her card and said, "Please come to tea."

When I got to London, I called her, and she invited me over the next day. She lived in Number 11 Downing Street and was married to the chancellor of the exchequer, Sir Geoffrey Howe. She was Lady Howe—not royalty, but something.

I went over there to Number 11, and we had tea and some cake she had left over from a couple of days before. I know it was left over because she told me half-apologetically as she cut it. There wasn't anyone else there. I had a good time talking about show business and politics with her for a couple of hours. She even freely talked about the focus of her life.

When I left, I had a new attitude about royalty. I kind of felt sorry for them. Sometime way back someone had won a war or made a lot of money, and now his great-great-great-grandchildren were a duchess or a duke or even a queen or king. It never looked like much fun from afar, and now that I had gotten a closer look, I was sure it wasn't. The more I thought about it, with all those people bowing to you all the time, the happier I was I was from Pittsburgh. I mean, I don't even like to be called Mr. Grodin.

Automobiles are like men; the less substantial they become, the more knocking they do.

—ANONYMOUS

Cars

WHEN I TURNED SIXTEEN, the age where I qualified for a driver's license, driving a car became my obsession. My dad had a Kaiser Traveler which he used for the family business and religiously kept away from me. A car for any sixteen-year-old, I guess, was so rare that those few among us who had access became almost magical folk heroes. Happily my close friend Jack Krongold had a red convertible of his own, so at least I was a backseat guy for my key teenage years.

When I reached twenty, I moved to New York, where owning a car completely disappeared from my mind for several reasons; mainly I couldn't afford to park it, let alone buy it.

Fifteen years later I arrived in Los Angeles to be on a soap opera for six months. Since it was Los Angeles, I had to have a car, and since it was the first time I'd really be making any money, I wanted to buy a Cadillac. When I was a boy growing up, only very successful people drove Cadillacs, and even though I wasn't very successful, I thought I had reached sufficient success to buy a Cadillac—a used one. Besides, I probably wanted to really make up in a big way for all my carless years.

A friend of a friend had a used-car lot, with all kinds of cars, and I went over there right away, looking for my Cadillac. It was a huge place—row after row of cars covering two city blocks. I was wandering around for about ten minutes before I saw it—the most beautiful car I had ever seen in my life: a 1958 white Cadillac convertible with red leather seats. I went to the friend's friend, and he followed me out onto the lot to see what I was so excited about. As we approached the car, he began to shake his head. "You don't want that car," he said. Not exactly what we're supposed to hear from used-car salesmen, but he was a friend's friend, and I was young, without much money.

"Why not?" I asked him as I climbed in and started to press buttons that made the seat move back and forth.

"She's a femme fatale," he said, "a siren, a looker who will break your heart." This guy was obviously not your average used-car salesman. He went on: "There's a blue Chevy over here I can really recommend."

"Wait a minute," I said, now hitting the button that made the seat go up and down. "What's the problem right here?"

He said, "I've seen it happen a million times. A kid like you buys a car like that and tries to make a new car out of it. It won't work, and it will end up costing you more money than you can think of."

Hitting the button that made the top go up and down, I said, "How much do you want for it?"

He said, "I'll give it to you for seven hundred dollars, no guarantees, and I'm telling you again not to take it."

"Sold," I said. I wrote him a check and drove it right off the lot, as he stood there shaking his head.

I loved it! I got myself a fancy hat and drove it all over Hollywood with the top down. I had more fun with it than anything I can remember . . . for about two weeks. Slowly, the problems started. I didn't take particular notice because I was making some money. The repair bills were $25 here, $50 there, $70 there. After a few more weeks it was $125 here, $175 there. Each time I was convinced that that would take care of that leak or that veering of the wheels or that fairly loud rattle. It didn't. I was doing exactly what the friend's friend had told me not to: trying to make a new car out of it. I couldn't seem to help myself. It always seemed like it was one repair job away from being perfect. Three thousand dollars' worth of repairs later, I was convinced I now had it all under control.

That afternoon the brakes failed, and I ran into the car in front of me. Nobody was hurt, thankfully. I had them fixed, and a week later they failed again, and I knocked down a telephone pole to avoid hurting anyone. I had them fixed again, but now I was starting to get a little wary. And poor.

One day, coming out of the place where I was staying, I noticed a large puddle of fluid under the car. I got in with my friend, another guy who wasn't going to win any prizes for brains about cars, and we headed down a steep hill, looking for a garage. Halfway down the hill the brakes failed again. We were about fifty yards away from Sunset Boulevard at rush hour. I jumped the curb, grazed a tree, and went right through a brick wall of a garage and stopped. Because the 1958 Cadillac was the most powerful thing around next to a Sherman tank, no one was hurt. I had it towed away, repaired, and the brakes fixed for the third time. After that I decided enough was enough. Fearful that the car would eventually kill someone, I decided to junk it, not sell it.

I drove it over to a junkyard and, after they promised me they would make scrap out of it, made a deal to sell my forty-five-hundred-dollar Cadillac for eight dollars.

It was a femme fatale, a siren, a looker that could break your heart—and everything else.

There is so much good in the worst of us,
And so much bad in the best of us,
That it hardly becomes any of us
To talk about the rest of us.

—EDWARD WALLIS HOCH

Judging

I'M NOT TOO BIG on judging. Every time someone starts talking about what's wrong with somebody I wonder and often say, "Why don't we criticize you or me or any of us here?" Obviously none of us is perfect, so why sit and judge others? I mean, really extreme bad stuff I can judge as much as the next guy, but on garden variety faults I'm not much of a judger.

There is one exception to all of this. There is one type I'm constantly judging because they drive me nuts. It's the authoritarian know-it-all, lots-of-rules kind of person.

I first ran into one early on in school. If ever someone like this belongs anywhere, it would be as a teacher in school, but I couldn't handle him there either. I was regularly thrown out of various classes for clashes with these control freaks.

My parents weren't like that, so maybe I was just shocked shortly after kindergarten that it felt like I had unwittingly entered the military. In fact, later *in* the military it didn't bother me at all. It was so extreme there I secretly thought it was funny. Of course, this was peacetime.

In my adult life these authoritarians have been my curse. I've done everything possible to avoid them. Sometimes it's impossible if they're in your family or you encounter them at work.

Work is the one place I've taken these people on. Most recently there was a producer working on a movie I did. The first time I saw this guy he was fairly quiet. It was a big meeting, so I didn't immediately spot what was in store.

One of the main characteristics of these people is their need to be right. I'm sure it's because they were once made to feel so wrong, so impotent, probably in childhood. I'm sympathetic to that, but *I* don't want to get beat up because they were subjected to childhood villains.

This particular producer, because of his need to win every point about anything, had alienated about fifty-eight people by the time the movie was over. He made haters out of some of the nicest people I've ever met in my life. His first direct assault on me came one morning, when we were shooting a huge train scene with a lot of extras. When I walked on the set, this guy looked at his watch, then at me, then announced, "I've been ready to shoot since eight-thirty." It was now nine, which was when I had been asked to arrive. I looked at him as though he were speaking Swahili to someone else and went about my business. There were other instances of this treatment toward me and everyone else on the picture. Eventually he was discreetly asked to be around less. That's usually what happens to these control freaks. They win some battles and then lose the war. The problem is they never seem to see the ultimate effect of what they're doing.

Sometimes I can feel sorrow and not anger toward them if I think deeply. Sadly I'm seldom that deep a thinker.

The best thing about animals is that they don't talk much.

—THORNTON WILDER

Animals

I HAVEN'T DONE AS well with animals as most people. On the positive side I find most dogs enormously touching and sweet. On the other hand, one of these sweet guys who actually was in my family once joined a dog pack and came after me snarling a long time ago. Our relationship was never the same. I'd still consider a dog in my life if it weren't for pooper-scoopers and shedding.

Cats are out. I'm allergic—heavily. They have their moments, but I've never quite settled in with all that back arching and hissing. The big cats—a lion, anyway—I can't even watch on television. Someone once said if something extremely strange for which there is no logical explanation is going on in your life, it's probably evidence of a previous existence. Judging by how quickly I change the channel when one of those lions comes on, I was once eaten by one; nothing less explains it. And if a lion comes out of a subway as it used to on those commercials—forget about it. I'm pretty quiet for a long time after that.

Oddly enough, my most memorable experience with animals was with, of all things, buffalo.

Very late one night I was walking home from filming a movie, and a herd of buffalo blocked my path. I was filming on the island of Catalina, which is some twenty-five miles off the coast of San Pedro, California. In the

1920s a movie company had gone over there to film a western and taken some buffalo with them. When they left, they left the buffalo.

I was staying a ten-minute boat ride from the main location. It was the only place near where we were filming that there were any kind of accommodations a city guy like me would be happy. The main location mostly offered tents and rooms with no roofs; the facility there was a boys' camp out of season. And while there were some rooms with roofs, all in all I said I'd take the ten-minute boat ride to the citylike accommodations. When I said that, I didn't know the buffalo herd lived over near my place.

A day's filming on a movie is generally at least twelve hours long. By the end of the day, and especially after a bumpy motorboat ride in the sea in total darkness (the driver held a spotlight in his hand), I was truly ready to go home. Once disembarked from the boat, I had a walk of about two hundred yards up a hill. I was always hungry and tired.

Prior to this I had seen a buffalo here and there on the island, always a fair distance away. I'd eyed them warily and kept going. I was told not to walk up and pet them or taunt them, which I hadn't planned to do anyway. I vaguely had heard stories of people who had tried stuff and were sorry, but I didn't know what they'd tried or how sorry they were. That was the extent of my information that night when I encountered the herd.

There must have been about a dozen of them directly blocking my path to home. No one was around. They seemed peaceful, but they were very big. I stood there in the darkness about thirty feet away and thought over the whole situation. They were scary; there was no question about that. I was also very tired and hungry; there was no question about that either. There was no phone and no one to consult. After about five minutes of thinking over all the possibilities, my hunger won out over my terror, and I casually, with enormous tension, walked through them and on home.

About six months later I was watching a documentary on television. For some reason I broke my tradition of changing channels when a lion appears and watched as one walked away from his pride, crossed a small stream, and was suddenly confronted by a couple of hyenas. The narrator explained that neither the lion nor the hyenas seemed all that interested in attacking each other, but after four more hyenas quickly showed up, that seemed to change. Now the lion was on the defensive. The narrator explained that it was very important he not let even one hyena get behind him. It seemed like he would only be able to keep them in front of him a little while longer when a large buffalo suddenly showed up on the scene. When the hyenas saw this guy, who looked very much like one of the twelve in my herd, they took off instantly. The narrator didn't explain why but let the picture speak for itself. As the hyenas were running in different directions, five or six more lions started to cross the stream to join the original lion and check out the action. Now there were about half a dozen lions and one buffalo. Again, the narrator explained, it was up to the buffalo now not to let any lion get behind him. For a couple of minutes the lions circled and the buffalo moved this way and that. The narrator explained that if one lion attacked, the rest would. But none of the lions seemed to want the job. Eventually they trotted away.

So I had just watched one buffalo disperse a pack of hyenas just by showing up and six or seven lions by moving to and fro a couple of times.

If I had seen that documentary before I had confronted that buffalo herd, I'd have gone hungry that night.

Kindness antedates psychiatry by hundreds of years; its antiquity should not lessen your opinion of its usefulness.

—ROSEWELL GALLAGER, M.D.

How Important Is Being Friendly?

SEVERAL YEARS AGO, AFTER a couple of relatively unpleasant experiences at work, I started to think about the importance of friendliness in life. Not that it always hasn't been right up there, but it started to hit head-on that if I, who was playing leading roles in movies, felt less than well treated, what must your average man and woman, who weren't in the movies, be treated like?

Oddly enough, prior to working in show business, I pretty much avoided human encounters in the workplace. I must have instinctively known something. I always sought jobs where there'd be no boss on the scene. I was a night watchman for the Pinkerton Detective Agency. I was a cabdriver. I worked for the post office, where if you sat on your stool and put your letters into the appropriate state slots, no one would even talk to you.

In my dealings with folks after I started to get out there a little, calling people, speaking to secretaries, etc., I often was told how nice it was to talk to me. I never thought that I was acting particularly nice, just normal. I mean, I knew "nice" people. They'd ask about your family at the drop of a hat and mean it. My mother's like that. She's a lot nicer than I am, and yet here I was being celebrated for my friendliness.

I started nosing around and got a widespread re-

137

sponse to my inquiries that in the workplace, particularly, people were rudely treated as a matter of normal, everyday life. The easy acceptance of this came, it seemed, from an awareness of stress at work that justified bosses' snapping, yelling, and worse. For a lot of people, home life didn't seem any better.

I sat around thinking about it for a couple of months, then contacted the friendliest person I knew, Carol Burnett, and told her all about what I was thinking. I wanted to go on national television and talk about the importance of friendliness. I didn't want to form an organization. Once I headed up the tenants' committee in a building I lived in, and that turned out to knock me out of the rest of life. So I didn't want to form an organization, just go out and talk about it nationally to see if it could be made into something of a higher priority—a consciousness raiser. Carol liked the idea even more than I did. She's a very optimistic person.

I started to prepare some literature and made some phone calls to get us booked on television. I called Phil Donahue, with whom I was acquainted. He was very nice but couldn't quite get a handle on what we could say about friendliness that could be a dynamic hour of television. I said I was working on it, and besides, I thought people would be interested in *anything* Carol Burnett had to say about anything. How she felt about the weather? Anything! Phil thought for a moment, then booked us into a large arena in Syracuse, New York. Carol and I went up there, talked about why it's important to be friendly for an hour, received rousing ovations and ten thousand pieces of mail.

I unfortunately thought it would be a good idea to have my mother and her roommate, Ann Baker, answer this mail. (This was before I realized the number would hit ten thousand.) My mother and Ann received an outpouring of emotion on the importance of the subject along with hundreds of religious books, tapes, etc. Their two-bedroom apartment came to look like the post office at Christmas. They responded to everything, but it's a subject I don't mention in their company today.

Next we were booked for ninety minutes on *The Merv Griffin Show*. Merv, we were shocked to learn right on the air, seemed to be *against* friendliness. In fairness, part of his attitude may have been motivated by wanting to make it a juicier show, but I have no question Merv, who is one of the friendliest people I know, was at least somewhat against being friendly. For example, he challenged me and a startled Carol: "What if a waiter spills soup on you in a restaurant—are you still friendly?" "Yes!" we answered with one voice. "The waiter probably feels worse than you do!" Merv clearly doubted that, implying it depended on how hot the soup was.

Amazingly to me, the experience with Merv was just the beginning of a counterattack. A writer for the *Village Voice* wrote a hostile piece that filled an entire page. He focused his attack not so much on friendliness or Carol, but mostly on me.

In all seriousness, he seemed to doubt that I really *was* all that friendly. He said he had seen me in a number of movies, and I struck him more as a guy who might take a doughnut off your plate when you weren't looking rather than a friendly guy. He said I looked like a doughnut thief.

Certain friends seemed deeply offended as well. They thought the whole subject was incredibly boring and felt if I wasn't quickly going to turn it into comedy, I should get the hell off the air and out of the newspapers right away.

Over the years some local organizations formed around the country to espouse the concept. Also over the years I've run into people at various functions who looked at me accusingly, wanting to know why I dropped my friendly "organization." I would try to explain it really wasn't an organization but a . . . No one seemed that interested in my explanation.

My most memorable experience of the whole endeavor came when I was asked to be the guest of honor for a convention of cosmetics executive women and give a speech on friendliness. I think I was invited because I did it for nothing or next to nothing. There was a small honorarium that I used to buy about one hundred little plaques with the phrase "We Are Friendly" on them, to be distributed at their luncheon. When I arrived for the event, I was introduced to various people and finally to a middle-aged man who, on being told my name and what I was doing there, looked like he wanted to kill me. My speech was received with minimal response, but afterward this man I had earlier met came over and apologized for his behavior. He said he had a rival perfume bottler named Charles Grodin, and that's who he thought I was. The fact that I looked ten years younger than he imagined I should and was also the guest of honor was more than he could take.

Looking back on the whole experience, I believe a lot more people appreciated this effort than were offended by it, but of course, on balance the country doesn't seem any friendlier.

Nobody ever said changing human nature was easy.

Happiness is beneficial for the body, but it is grief that develops the powers of the mind.

—MARCEL PROUST

Doctors

RECENTLY AN OLDER FRIEND was talking about a party she had gone to and said pridefully, "The place was filled with doctors." For another generation that definitely would have been a place to be. I was surprised at my own hostility toward the comment.

My first memory of a doctor is from childhood, when our family doctor, Dr. Lebeau, came to our house, felt my forehead, and then stood by my bed and talked with my mother. It was nice.

As a teenager I remember a classmate of mine saying he planned to go on to college to study medicine. He then told me why. Helping people was about his fifth reason, well after getting to see women naked. I was startled.

I remember in my twenties having a family doctor who was so aggressively brusque we all tried to take it as kind of a humorous personality. After a couple of years there was no way to take it as anything but aggressively brusque, and we moved on.

For several years after that my experience with doctors, thankfully, was infrequent. In my forties I had to have a couple of things checked out. Various instruments were put into various orifices. I must have had an incredibly detached attitude because it never even entered my mind that maybe they would find something that wouldn't be such good news. Happily they didn't.

As time went by, it suddenly struck me that I didn't have to feel sick to be sick, maybe even to be really sick. That's when my trouble started. I told my doctor, a very nice man who had a picture of Henry Fonda on a treadmill in his office, that suddenly I was becoming nervous about the whole health thing. There had been some shocking illnesses around me. Also, I was getting to the age where my father had died. My doctor suggested that if I was concerned about it, I could come in for checkups every few months, rather than once a year. I chose not to come in at all. Eventually that changed, and I do creep into a doctor's office every so often. I'm no longer plagued by the subject of health, nor am I detached.

Getting more in touch with the subject has now got me more in touch with the personalities and characters of the doctors. For myself I have no complaints. I have generally been treated well. One exception was going to a doctor once who wanted to know how many women I had slept with in my life. I honestly didn't see the relevance of the question to the purpose of my visit and told him. He couldn't explain the relevance but only commented that there were a lot of weirdos in show business. (I guess meaning me.) I answered there were a lot of weirdos in his field as well (definitely meaning him). We parted shooting each other suspicious looks.

My real problem with the medical profession has come in recent years in dealing with doctors of friends and family.

One specific doctor dealing with a family member with a terminal illness has unfortunately made me wary of the whole profession. This man had to be the single most insensitive human I've ever met in my life. We were dealing with a family catastrophe, and this guy had the manner of a foreman on a chain gang. He was mean. He was insensitive. He was a bully, and he was talking to a dying person surrounded by loved ones. Happily today he no longer speaks to sick humans but, by his own choice, is confined to a lab. A test tube could sense his unpleasantness.

There are many instances of doctor insensitivity that have rolled around me since. Anyone who has been to some doctors I'm sure has his own list. I've tried to understand it. Being on call while you're asleep would certainly make me edgy. Being asked to be on duty forty-eight consecutive hours or whatever that lunatic rule is would certainly not prepare me to be everyone's favorite. Seeing every possible thing that can happen to a person would probably make me less sensitive than if I had seen nothing. Still, when I was given the name of a thoracic surgeon to call about a possible lung cancer of someone extremely close to me, and the doctor said in a snide tone, "I hear you're on the edgy side. I mean, this is not an ongoing heart attack!" I paused for a moment to keep my edginess from exploding into something worse, then replied, "Cancer is enough to get my attention."

The horror stories go on. I have understanding for the stress of doctors. Some obviously handle it better than others. I know all professions are filled with sensitive and insensitive people. It's just that when you're ill, especially terminally, a little insensitivity goes a long way. And that goes for you doctors' secretaries, too!

I much prefer a compliment, insincere or not, to sincere criticism.

—PLAUTUS

Accepting Criticism

IT SEEMS A PERSON'S ability to accept criticism is directly related to his ability to grow. It also seems that most criticism comes from without. It's the rare person who will sit around and criticize himself in a healthy way—rather than unhealthy, where you punish yourself at any opportunity.

A friend once said, "I hope I grow as I get older because I'd hate to be an old baby."

Anyone might be initially defensive or embarrassed when hearing criticism, but I've worked hard to get to the point where eventually I'm actually grateful if someone offers a criticism I can accept as valid—*stung* but grateful.

I've heard more than one person who really has been guilty of rough stuff try to deflect criticism by shrugging and saying, "Well, nobody's perfect," or, "We all make mistakes." Not much chance for growth there.

I've found that people who have had a lot of criticism (particularly unfair) in childhood have a very tough time accepting *any* as adults. Some even hear criticism when none is there. I once casually remarked in a restaurant, "Gee, it's chilly in here." My date snapped, "I guess that's my fault!" She had made the reservation, but still . . .

I think we should give ourselves the benefit of the doubt, but if you hear the same knock more than a few times over the years—well, 'fess up.

If we could change half the things wrong with us, the world would be a noticeably better place.

The English country gentleman galloping after a fox—the unspeakable in full pursuit of the uneatable.

—OSCAR WILDE

For Women on Dealing with Sports on Television

FIRST OF ALL, THE relationship of men to sports might be analogous to the relationship of a mother to her first-born—nothing to be messed with.

Years ago I couldn't help but notice that my emotional ups and downs seemed to be startlingly affected by the ups and downs of my sports teams. Of course, if I were an owner, a manager, or a player, that would make sense, but I am a fan, no more or less devoted than the average fan—which means winning or losing can feel like life and death. Actually in matters of life and death I tend to be a little less emotional.

Once when I was a very young fellow, I was walking down the street feeling on top of the world. After a few minutes I wondered why. I had no money, no job, no prospects, and yet I was moving in my version of Gene Kelly in *Singin' in the Rain*. The New York Giants football team had just won a game.

I once asked a psychiatrist friend why people identified so much with their teams. He said, generally speaking, people's egos couldn't sufficiently be gratified by what they accomplished in life, so they attach themselves to something bigger than they are—their team. The catch, of course, is when the team loses, you lose, too. I've found that when my team wins, it puts me in touch with all the good feelings I have about life and myself; when they lose—don't ask.

So, ladies, when you look in that room and see us riveted to that TV screen, try not to be too bugged. I honestly believe that a relationship is seriously helped by a supportive attitude toward this particular neurosis. Try it. You'd be amazed at how much nicer your partner might be in those few hours a week when there isn't a sporting event on television.

Trust everybody, but cut the cards.

—FINLEY PETER DUNNE

Broken Promises

I DON'T KNOW IF more promises are broken in show business than in other businesses or in life in general. I do know that in show business "yes" means "maybe" and "maybe" means "no." I once wrote a movie that a producer said he was going to do. A few weeks later I was told he wasn't. I called him and said, "I thought you said you were going to do it." He literally answered, "When I said I was going to do it, that didn't mean I was going to do it." I took a moment to make sure I heard right, then asked, "What did it mean?" He said, "It meant I was going to do it if—" He then listed about ten ifs. Around the sixth if, I started to get very tired.

Professional broken promises are one thing. Life's are the ones that really hurt, and I believe we're all guilty of those.

In relationships, on those first dates, that's where the unspoken promises are made. We're at our best, our most careful, and we seem to buy the other's act and even our own.

Nobody's as wonderful as on that first meeting, and here I believe the personal and professional are the same.

157

How many times have you said or heard someone else say, "I just met the best woman, man, teacher, boss," etc.? There's a million of them.

Maybe we should all be made to wear sweat shirts for any first meeting, saying on them, "This is me at my best. After a while a lot of stuff comes out you probably won't like."

At least later it would cut down on the shock.

Beware of all enterprises that require new clothes.

—HENRY DAVID THOREAU

Fashion

I NEVER UNDERSTOOD THE reason for fashion. Who needs some guy in Europe to decide what we should wear? I just don't get it. When it's cold, I dress warm. When it's warm, I dress light. I like certain colors. For years I seemed to irritate people with my desire to stay in the brown family. Now I move it around a little: an occasional dark blue, maybe some gray—nothing really out there.

Recently I bought a tartan plaid thing really because I couldn't figure out if it was a shirt or a jacket, and it was my high school colors. I don't wear it, though.

When I was young and poor, I bought my sports jackets for meetings at Sun drugstores. They sold them for $3.99. I'm not kidding. I never got a job when wearing one, but I didn't get a job when I didn't wear one either.

I've always been amazed how these guys in Europe could get women to wear their skirts as high up as they decided. What if some nut over there got in charge and said, "Don't wear skirts at all?" Would women have just gone around in panties? Actually, hot pants came close.

On second thought, maybe there's something to fashion after all.

There is nothing as stupid as an educated man if you get off the thing he was educated in.

—WILL ROGERS

Teachers

RECENTLY I WAS ASKED to do a public service announcement on behalf of teachers, and I surprised the people who asked me and even myself a little when I said, "That wouldn't be a good idea, because generally I don't like teachers." Obviously there are brilliant, wonderful, sensitive, humane teachers all over the place. Unfortunately I've almost never run into them.

Basically I've run into a lot of teachers who are arrogant, superior, and boring. Even though I was a high honor student and class president, I almost quit high school because of this. It drove me nuts! I had a teacher in ninth grade, an older, tall, heavyset woman who would write the words "Pittsburgh, Pennsylvania" on the blackboard so slowly that by the time she got to the P in "Pennsylvania" I had the shakes. Besides, I knew how to spell Pittsburgh, Pennsylvania, when I was in the third grade! After she started to teach us stuff I knew in sixth grade, I went to her and said maybe I was in the wrong class. She didn't even respond. I wasn't the only one in the class that felt this way. There were about a dozen of us who became major fidgeters.

I've just seen too many teachers with superior attitudes. Obviously they know more about their subject than students do, but why flaunt it? I once had to learn to ride a horse for a role on a TV western. I went out to

165

some stables and ran into a first-class arrogant bully. This guy could ride a horse—big deal! I had to learn in a hurry, so I decided to ignore the ridiculing attitude. Besides, the instructor down the street probably wasn't any different.

In grammar school, where corporal punishment was allowed, the third-grade teacher, Miss Kilb, would smack us across our hands with a ruler when we acted like eight-year-olds. In woodshop Mr. Pomesano was permitted to have us come up to the front of the class, reach over, touch our toes, and then whack us on the rear with a large wooden paddle—for talking. The single-file, no-talking rule always felt penitentiarylike to me, too.

In high school Mr. Kennedy would regularly throw me out of class for asking too many questions. I will admit that while everyone was subjected to these restrictions, it clearly always seemed to bother me the most. It seems I fluctuated from having no idea what they were talking about to having learned it years ago. It was a mess.

In my adult life I've been thrown into some class situations obviously against my will. My wife asked me to go to a Lamaze class with her when she was pregnant, so of course, I went. When we got there, the instructor announced she had a show on cable TV and might want to interview some of us later. She then asked each person to stand, say his name, and announce why he was there. I was first. I said my name and that I was there because my wife had asked me to come. The teacher smiled weakly and stared at me. During the course of the class I asked three separate times what exactly was the purpose of Lamaze. I never really got a clear answer, and neither did my wife, who, you'll be relieved to hear, is not as confrontational as I am. When she did go into labor practicing the breathing they teach you, the only thing we really thought helped was the pain-killing shot.

Later, after the baby was born, we went to a CPR class. This time I asked for just a private lesson, figuring I'd behave myself better. I was told the lesson would take over an hour. I said to my wife if it takes over an hour to explain what to do when someone stops breathing, I'm going to get too much information and probably won't remember what I really need to know. The instructor, a nice young woman, spent the first half hour telling us where every body organ was located and the next forty-five minutes on some other stuff. If you should ever start to choke, pray you're not with me because I'd have no idea how to help you. However, I could tell you where your kidneys are.

Before the baby was born, we took a tour of the hospital. The guide was helpful, clear, sensitive, not superior—an equal. I was shocked. Here was the teacher I had been looking for all my life. When it was over, I went up to her and thanked her so profusely she was clearly startled. I mean, I almost kissed her ring.

If I'd had teachers like this in my life, maybe I wouldn't have been a college dropout. I'd probably know some bigger words and have a much deeper understanding of just what the hell life is about. Also, you wouldn't have to read angry pieces like this.

In ancient days the most celebrated precept was "Know thyself"; in modern times it has been supplanted by the more fashionable maxim, "Know thy neighbor, and everything about him."

—ANONYMOUS

Going Deeper

SOMETIMES I CAN'T HELP it, I try to go deeper. I'm not saying my deeper is that deep, but it's a direction I head into on occasion.

It usually happens when people start talking about furniture. A table. A lamp. A chair. A sofa. I'm OK for a while, a very short while, and then I start to get anxious and dive deeper like a submarine under attack. I'll start seemingly harmlessly at a pause and say something like "So how ya doin'?" and when someone says, "Fine," I dive into "I mean, what's going on with you?" Usually I see a flicker of panic cross the other person's eyes, wondering exactly how deep he's going to be forced to go. He usually counters with something like "Oh, I've been real busy, a lot of work and stuff." I'll nod and then might hit him with something like "How ya feeling?" Once getting past "Fine," I try to get him to reveal what he really feels, even though I'm not always anxious to go down these roads myself, but furniture talk drives me there.

Generally speaking, I get the feeling people don't want to go deeper because deeper often means sadder. And no one would choose to get sadder right in the middle of a furniture conversation, so I am looked on with mixed feelings. People appreciate my caring but can ultimately resent me for it, too.

171

Some people have found me strange and hostile because of my unwillingness to go in for furniture talk. Partly, I guess, because I dive in with my how-ya-really-doing stuff always as a non sequitur. It's not that easy to get from chairs to "How ya doin'?"

People don't like non sequiturs. It clearly implies lack of interest in the present subject. So the chair conversants always whip their heads around at me and give me a look you don't want to get.

I've actually gotten better at controlling myself. I try to stay away from non sequiturs and depth when inappropriate. I have to admit I don't have as much fun going out now as I used to, but at least the people around me seem more relaxed.

If we could see ourselves as others see us, we would never speak to them again.

—ANONYMOUS

If We Could See Ourselves

Sees Self As:	Seen by Others As:
1. Helpful. Do anything for you. Smart.	1. Arrogant. Know-it-all.
2. Eccentric. Obsessive. Bright.	2. Crazy. Self-indulgent. Dummy.
3. Cheerful. Friendly. Loving. Bright.	3. A tyrant. A phony. Stupid.
4. Private. Careful.	4. Neurotic. Control freak.
5. Outgoing. Speaks his mind.	5. Insensitive loudmouth.

Some of the ways we see ourselves, of course, are similar to what are seen by others, but we tend to give ourselves a break. After all, how could anyone want to get up in the morning if he saw himself as an insensitive loudmouth?

We never really know what's in another person's heart or mind. We may think we do, but like they say, until you've walked in those shoes. . . .

Let's give the other person a break and at least call it:

1. Helpful know-it-all
2. Eccentric dummy
3. Cheerful phony
4. Private control freak
5. Outgoing loudmouth

Sweet are the uses of adversity.

—WILLIAM SHAKESPEARE

Unreturned Phone Calls

I RETURN ALL PHONE calls I get because I so don't like not having my calls returned.

A lot of people unfortunately don't think this is such a big deal. They'll say, "I was busy," "I didn't have anything to report to you," "I was waiting until next week to see if—" I say, "Don't wait. Return calls as soon as possible."

People can take real trips over not having their calls returned, and none of them is pleasant. Often, whether true or not, the message seems to be "You're not important enough for me to return your call. Who cares that you called?" These unreturned phone calls inevitably will coincide with other setbacks we all experience, so they just heighten the negativity. Bad, bad news.

I had a friend who wasn't so hot at returning phone calls. He had a lot of reasons, but basically, if he didn't feel like returning your call, he wouldn't. Another friend had a great success and wanted his nearest and dearest around to celebrate with him. The non-phone-call-returning friend heard about the party and said he'd come as well, assuming the response would be an automatic "Sure, love to see you." Instead, the message was "There are not enough chairs at the table." I told my startled friend this had something to do with not returning phone calls. It was the first time he realized the impact of his insensitivity.

I've also seen resentment caused by people asking friends for major favors by having their secretaries call.

This phone stuff is a tricky business. It's much more loaded than some people seem to be aware. Be aware.

Wisdom consists in being able to distinguish among dangers and make a choice of the least harmful.

—NICCOLÒ MACHIAVELLI

Answering Services

MANY PEOPLE COMPLAIN ABOUT answering services, and I have, too. The complaints range from "They never answer" to "They pick up before I do." This has bothered me, but what bothers me more is when they ask people what the nature of their call is or "Who are you with?" No matter how many times I tell my services over the years not to do that, just take the name, they will sometimes give me a message and say, "He said it was a personal call." Then, of course, there are the names of the callers themselves, mostly recognizable but sometimes . . . well, you know. Still, all in all, I have seldom changed services. I figure after a while there's not much difference, and I'm strangely grateful for the messages that get through.

When you're in a no-news-is-good-news phase, you don't want any messages, but my service always seems sad for me when they don't have any. I've thought of saying, "I'm glad there are no messages," but they probably wouldn't believe me—probably think I'm just putting up a brave front. Then I'd have to deal with their feeling even more sorry for me. So I keep quiet.

Under significant pressure from family and friends, I have resisted the main alternative to answering services—answering machines. It's not just that I don't want to go through having the machine on by mistake when

183

I'm home, the shouting out of "Hold on a minute," and the playing out of the message and the beep while the caller waits. It's more than that. My worst nightmare is somehow Hitler *is* alive, he gets my number and leaves me a heinous message. In my calmer moments I know Hitler won't call, but even a lot less villainous people than Hitler, disembodied, speaking to me in the safe haven of my den could make me sorry I had a machine. I know all of this is highly unlikely, and yet still I feel I get through life a little more comfortably with my service.

So if you ever call me and no one picks up, or when someone does and asks you who you're with or the nature of your call, I'm really sorry. Think about my Hitler thing and forgive me.

Three may keep a secret if two of them are dead.

—BENJAMIN FRANKLIN

Secrets

I HAVE ALWAYS BEEN a fairly secretive person. I hesitate to say why because it's kind of a secret. Actually I've been this way for so long it's hard to remember why sometimes. But I'll try.

In certain instances it's obvious. If someone tells his best friend that his boss is a big jerk, and that's not treated as a secret, well . . . For years I found it necessary to intersperse my conversations with friends with the phrase "between us," "stays in this room," etc. What may be an obvious secret to one person isn't necessarily to another. I've backed off that a bit since one friend said when my name comes up in conversation, she tenses and forgets what she can or can't say past admitting she knows me.

Another friend was told something mean that was said about her behind her back. The person who gave her the information did so because her husband had told her, "Knowledge is power." In this case knowledge was just depression.

Ironically the most famous secretive person of our time, Howard Hughes, chose to communicate all his secrets in secret memos which were later discovered in a secret warehouse in Hollywood. These were all put into a book which I read.

I'm sure all of Mr. Hughes's secrets seemed worth

keeping at the time. The most interesting chapter in the book contained all the memos he sent to and received from his right-hand man in planning a huge party in Las Vegas. Most of these secret memos were about who should be invited or not and why and why not. That chapter gave me almost as big a headache as it gave Mr. Hughes's right-hand man. The biggest secret revealed in the book was that Howard Hughes appears to have been nuts.

Maybe that's why I'm so secretive.

. . . when I was at home, I was in a better place. . . .

—WILLIAM SHAKESPEARE

Fear of Flying

FOR YEARS THE ONE great fear in my life was flying. I would do anything to avoid flying. I would take trains, buses, or drive great distances. Primarily my fear had to do with taking off in a huge jet thundering down the runway. That's not to say that when we were up, I was Lucky Lindy or anything, but those takeoffs were really it. Even though they only took a minute or so, thinking about that minute used up days.

In flight I jumped when the captain came on with his "Ladies and gentlemen." I always thought he was going to say, "Ladies and gentlemen, I'm sorry to inform you I have no idea how to keep this huge steel monster in the sky any longer." Instead, of course, he'd be pointing out some damn lake on our left.

Amazingly all this ended suddenly one day when a friend of mine suggested I think of all that noise the jet makes when it thunders down the runway as working *for* me, not against. Strangely it seemed like a good idea. The next time I got myself into the inevitable situation of having to fly, as the plane thundered down the runway, I heard all the noise as *for* rather than against, and stunningly to me, I was fine.

Now it seemed the louder, the better. This led to all kinds of reassuring thoughts like "If it really was dangerous, would the captain and his men be doing it?" Of course not! Suddenly all the statistics about it being more dangerous in a car or even your own bathtub made sense.

It's all how you look at it.

More die in the United States of too much food than of too little.

—JOHN KENNETH GALBRAITH

Leftovers

I'VE GOT A THING about leftovers. It must have come from childhood. If there are any leftovers in the refrigerator, I can't eat new food unless I have a plan for those leftovers. This is not a sacrifice for me because I prefer leftovers. To me new food is just food waiting to be left over.

I think leftovers taste better, but even if they didn't, I have to take care of them before moving on. Of course, my preoccupation with this doesn't thrill my wife. In fairness, the situation is worse than I've described. I try to push the leftovers, not usually very successfully because most people want new food. I describe their tastiness. I tell people they're better than new food. I get as aggressive as I can get without people asking me to leave my own house.

Of course, all this comes from lines from my youth like "Finish everything on your plate. There are people starving in India." That really compelled me to finish up as a boy. It doesn't make any sense now when I think of it.

Nobody hungry anywhere cares about anyone but himself cleaning up a plate, or maybe my mother meant you're fortunate to have food, so eat it all. It seems I'm still taking that advice. No food goes to waste around me. Luckily I'm fortunate enough to have an exercise machine as well.

April 1. This is the day upon which we are reminded of what we are on the other three hundred and sixty-four.

—MARK TWAIN

Holidays

I CELEBRATE NO HOLIDAYS of any kind unless a family member or close friend puts in a personal request, and then I will respond with a funny hat and a tooter on New Year's Eve or sing "Happy Birthday" with the best of them. No one would spot me for a ringer.

All of these special days suggest to me that the rest of them aren't. For years I have annoyed people with this point of view.

I know the concept is that you should be a good son to your mother every day but on Mother's Day do something special. In practice there's a lot of ignoring going on all year and attempts to compensate for it on the special day.

While I am chastised for ignoring holidays, I try to make an effort to be a 365-holidays-a-year guy. I'm sure I fail on a regular basis. People seldom get what they really need from others.

I have a friend, an alcoholic, who tries to celebrate something every day in an effort to get everyone to join him in a toast. "It's exactly three weeks since we last saw each other!" he will exclaim as he raises his glass high.

In spite of my antiholiday position, I must admit I do have a favorite. That's Thanksgiving. I like it so much I manage to have turkey and stuffing about fifty times a year.

Of course, the real problem here, as we all know, is hardly anyone celebrates these holidays for what they're supposed to be about. I don't remember the last time I heard the word "Pilgrims" during Thanksgiving or "Jesus" at a Christmas party. A small percentage of us mourn the war dead on Memorial Day. The rest of us watch baseball games or go to the beach.

As a boy, because my family did it, I fasted on Yom Kippur, the Day of Atonement, but I wasn't thinking about atonement, just that when it got dark, I could eat the apple pie in the oven.

For millions, Easter is definitely a time to dress up, not celebrate the Resurrection.

New Year's Eve is when I'm a real party pooper. I'm asleep when the new year comes in. This is probably my least favorite holiday as it brings to mind the passage of time, and what the hell does "Auld Lang Syne" mean anyway?

Any fool can criticize, condemn and complain, and most fools do.

—DALE CARNEGIE

Complaining

I GOT IN A cab recently and asked the driver if he would please close the right front window. He manually put it up, then bitterly complained, "Before this car I was driving a 'seventy-seven car, and it had automatic window controls. This is an 'eighty-six, and it doesn't!"

As we got to a difficult intersection, I apologetically said, "I should have told you to go a block left where there's a light." He responded in a surprisingly petulant manner, "Yeah, well, unless you tell me, I wouldn't know." After a few minutes on a crowded freeway he moaned, "Couple of lousy drivers can mess up a freeway. It's Saturday! They shouldn't be driving!"

We all complain. It's human nature, so the issue must be how much and under what circumstances is it OK. I guess it's OK if you're doing it with another person, and you're both in there wailing away, but watch out if you're the only one. Chances are the other person wishes you'd stop, before his headache sets in. I've found a kind of logy, depressed feeling comes over me from the unrelenting complainers. I mean, the ones who after you say "hello" say, "Oh, what a day I've had," then proceed to lay it on you.

Personally I try to go light on complaints except sometimes maybe to my poor wife, and then I try never to complain about her, so she'll have more patience with my other complaints.

Overall, I think it's helpful to keep perspective. How was your day compared with an earthquake victim's, for example? That's fairly inhibiting. Also, keep complaints short, interesting, and funny if possible. A lot of people have turned that notion into careers as professional comedians.

I think the biggest reason I'm not much of a complainer is that I work hard to do things that make me feel good. That way, when the bad stuff hits, I've got all my good stuff to fall back on before much of a complaint can set in. It often works.

I am a believer in punctuality, though it makes me very lonely.

—ANONYMOUS

Punctuality

I SO BELIEVE IN being on time that sometimes I am an early arriver, which can be worse than being late.

Punctuality, or the lack of it, to me is a big deal. Like unreturned phone calls, it takes on larger ramifications for some of us. Some people want to be "fashionably late," which I'm told is ten minutes. I've known people who can be a half hour to an hour late and think nothing of it. If this is at a large party, I agree, but when you're sitting alone in a restaurant waiting for someone . . .

I'm always on time because I find it insulting not to be. People set aside a particular time to see me, and if I'm late, it clearly implies that I think my time is more valuable than theirs. Of course, you can always find some excuse, and people do, but I try not to be involved with people who are always offering excuses about anything.

For me, punctuality, or lack of it, becomes a more harrowing experience if it's someone close who's late, because then, of course, your imagination takes over.

My most memorable experience in this area came when my daughter was younger and borrowed my car for a drive in the country. She got lost, returned about two hours later than expected, and found me standing in the middle of the dark road in front of my house.

I remember as a teenager coming home at 5:00 A.M.,

getting out of a car, and seeing my mother looking down at me from her bedroom window. What goes around comes around.

My worst experience came again with my daughter when she was sixteen. I went to meet a plane she was on, and she wasn't there. I waited and scanned the terminal for an hour, then went home, made some calls, and learned she had boarded the plane. After about two horrible hours of calling police, hospitals, etc., she turned up. She was somehow in another waiting area I had missed. She had then gotten involved in a fascinating conversation with someone about . . . By that time I couldn't hear what she was saying as my emotions made me deaf.

I guess the moral of all this is please be on time if you're meeting someone who cares about you or even someone who doesn't.

There aren't any embarrassing questions—only embarrassing answers.

—CARL ROWAN

Impotence

I WAS ONCE ON an afternoon talk show on television where a doctor was explaining how you could tell if you were impotent or not. As the discussion began, I realized I didn't even know what impotence was. I wasn't sure whether it meant you couldn't, as they say, "perform," or did it mean you could "perform" but you couldn't have a baby? Well, I guess most of you know this already, but for those of you like me, it means you can't "perform." Of course, you could still "perform" and not have babies, but this discussion was just about "performing" and how to find out if the reason you couldn't, if you couldn't, was psychological or physical.

The doctor said the way to find out if you could have an erection was when you went to sleep at night, apply however many postage stamps you needed to circle your penis. Since it's normal during the course of the night for a man to have at least one erection in his sleep, the stamps should have parted by morning. If they did, you'd know your problem was psychological. If the stamps were unbroken, it meant your problem was physical. So you could find out if your problem was physical or psychological. He didn't say what to do when you found out. I figured, whichever it was, you'd still have postage on your penis, so you could always mail it to the lab for further study.

He also said the temperature of the testicles was important on the subject of potential fertility, but I can't remember if he said to try to keep them on the warm or cold side. He also said something about Jockey shorts as regards cold or warm, but I can't remember which they did for you either. I do remember he said that every woman, along with her vagina, has a tiny, tiny, almost invisible penis, and every man has a similar-sized tiny, tiny vagina to go with his penis. By that time the whole subject was starting to make me so uncomfortable I really didn't hear much of anything else.

"Be yourself!" is about the worst advice you can give some people.

—TOM MASEFIELD

Rats, Four-Legged and Two

I HAVE LIVED IN some extremely meager, at best, places. When I first came to New York, I lived in a hotel in a single room with no window and a bathroom down the hall. I graduated up to a cold-water flat on the Lower East Side with the bathtub in the kitchen and the bathroom down the hall. My mother, when visiting, would not enter either building.

Ironically the only places I ever encountered rats, the four-legged kind, were not in these buildings but in very expensive surroundings, later when I was doing better. Oh, when I first did summer stock in Madison, Ohio, there was a rat in my mattress, but he was dead.

Here, I am talking about close encounters of the first kind—me and the rats, big ones, in the same expensive place.

My most memorable rat encounter was when I went on the only vacation I've ever taken. I was staying with a friend at a posh resort in Saint Martin in the Caribbean. It was a highly recommended place. "Robert Redford stays there" was the line from the travel agent that sold me. We had a beautiful suite on the second floor. One evening we were sitting in the living room, talking, when I looked past my friend and saw a large rat on the outside of the screen of the bedroom window. I casually got up, walked into the bedroom, whacked the screen with a hard-cover copy of Joseph Califano's *Governing America*, heard the rat fall to the ground below, and returned to my seat in the living room. I was in a state of shock.

"What was that?" my friend asked. "Lizard," I said. She hadn't bothered to turn around during my move. Suddenly I saw a big rat move quickly from the hallway to under the sofa where my friend was sitting. She heard it, saw my face, hopped up on top of the sofa, and said, simply, "What?"

"OK," I said, "we have a rat under the sofa." "OK," I said again, for no reason. I then really surprised myself as a Burt Lancaster type of guy started to emerge from me. "You stay on the sofa," I said, in full command. I went to the phone. I sat with my feet on the floor—not on the sofa. Burt Lancaster wouldn't sit with his feet on the sofa, tucked under—not in hundreds of movies and not in life either, I bet.

The operator answered. "Hello," I said easily, "we have a rat in our room." "A rat?" the operator said. "Yes," I said easily. "Could you send someone over here right away?" He murmured something in a language I didn't understand. I said, "Right away, please." He spoke foreign again and hung up. My friend, trying to fit into the role of Lancaster's woman, easily asked, "They said they'd send someone right away?" I nodded.

After five minutes of nervous looks back and forth, my friend suggested I call the operator again. He said, "Yes. The gentleman with the rat." Someone was, in fact, on the way. "What would he do when he got here?" I asked. "He will be there very soon, and you will see for yourself, my friend." "He's done this before? He knows what to do?" "You will see," he said. "He'll be arriving right away?" I asked—aware I was slipping from Burt Lancaster toward Pinky Lee—and not caring. He muttered something foreign again and hung up. A few minutes passed as my friend and I intermittently smiled and stared at each other.

There was an authoritative rap on the door. I opened it, and a small black man, about forty, stood there smiling at me. "You have a rat." He grinned. "Yes," I said as he entered, carrying a flashlight. He cheerfully asked me where it was. "Under the sofa," I answered. He then suggested my friend and I go into the bedroom and close the lattice doors. I sent my friend in and said I'd stay out there with him. Personally, I, of course, would have liked to have left the island, but I'm interested in protecting my opinion of myself, so I opted to stay with him out there in rat land.

The man, grinning widely, was warming to the task as he, appearing as though he did this about eighty times a day, whacked the couch with his flashlight while we both watched, transfixed. Nothing happened. Grinning, he quickly pushed the couch completely off its spot. No rat. He then pulled at it. It turned out to be a sofa bed. A sofa bed, like most sofa beds, that was incredibly hard to pull out and almost impossible to push back in. It revealed nothing but some moldy-looking Halloween-type candy on the blanket. "Rat food," I thought, but even a rat wouldn't have been able to get at it. He then did a thorough examination of the living room. No rat. He grinned and told me that even if you had a rat, a rat is only interested in food, he wouldn't bother you, he just looks for food, and you can hear him looking and eating. He grinned again as though this would reassure me. Living in New York City, my impression of the range of what rats eat was a little different, but we were having a pretty fair amount of trouble understanding each other, so I just suggested we continue our search of the place.

We moved back into a complete and thorough exam-

ination of the bathroom, hall, and closet area where the
rat had first appeared. No rat. Nothing. The guy grinned
at me again and said there was no rat, but to make me
feel better—it was very late now—first thing in the morning they would put poison in the place, but now all was
OK. He grinned. No rat.

His logic eluded me. I had the same set of facts he
did, and my conclusion was there was a rat now locked
in the bedroom with my friend. I shared my thought
with him. He looked at me quizzically, a little like I had
touches of Sherlock Holmes. I told my friend we were
coming in. She was perched up on the bed. I explained
the situation and suggested now she and I leave the bedroom and let this gentleman do his thing. She nodded
uneasily, and as she gingerly stepped off the bed, the rat
ran across the room from behind a night table. She
leaped back up on the bed. We all stared at each other.
I suggested, once again, that my friend and I repair to the
living room. Everyone agreed. She tried the move again
cautiously, then quickly flew out the door, and there we
were in the living room as the rat and our guy with his
flashlight were in their now-enclosed arena.

There was no exit from that bedroom now, and yet
my friend was back perched on the sofa, and I, sad to
admit, was perched up beside her. There was only silence, at this point, from the bedroom. I wondered about
the modus operandi of our rescuer since he was armed
only with a flashlight. Was he going to just shine that
beam on the rat, question him, get him to admit he was,
in fact, a rat, not registered and give himself up? No, for
immediately we heard a loud crash—what against what
no one could know. What then followed for the next ten
minutes can only be described as a series of unfathom-
able sounds. Whackings, bangings, smashings, crash-
ings, thumpings, divings . . . dead silence . . . heavy

breathing. Now, more distinct sounds: a bed being overturned, bureaus being shoved fiercely this way and that,
then more whacking, crashing . . . silence. Our guy,
sweating pretty good, suddenly opened the door a crack
and, wild-eyed, looked around the living room. He spots
a can of Raid, grabs it, and is back in there. "A can of
Raid?" I thought. "Raid kills things rats eat. It doesn't
kill rats."

Now squirting was added to the crashing, banging,
smashing. A couple more wild bureau moves, another
bed being overturned, more squirts, a few more unfath-
omable sounds, and our guy emerges again—running
wildly around the living room and kitchen, shouting,
"Weapon! Weapon!" My friend pointed to a lot of weap-
onlike kitchen utensils, which he ignored and ran back
into the fray—empty-handed. A few of the shouts and
hisses really sounded now like they were coming from
the rat. Was the whole thing turning in some bizarre
fashion? Had our guy radically underestimated what he
was dealing with? I faintly remembered something from
childhood about a rat that was cornered. I couldn't remember what the rest of it was, but I had a quick fantasy
of a six-foot-one-inch rat emerging, crossing over to the
coffee table, lighting up a cigarette, looking at us a moment, and casually leaving. There now had been no
sound at all from the bedroom for about a minute. We
looked at each other in confusion. Should we call for
more help?

We waited. Then the door opened, and our guy,
shirtless, dripping wet, exhausted, stood in the doorway
and looked at us. We stared at him. "What is it? What
happened?" I finally asked. He grinned, kind of a weak,
tired grin. He beckoned us to come in and take a look.
"You got him?" my friend asked. He grinned again. We
very cautiously moved toward the bedroom. Mattresses

had been overturned, barricades had been constructed, one set of springs was vertical against the wall, the lamps were on the floor—a complete upside-down, inside-out shambles of a room. A battle to the end had been fought here. We looked around. He pointed behind one of the barricades of bureaus. I peered around. There he was, lying there on his side, eyes open, not squished, not banged around, perfect, almost beautiful—a defeated warrior. I felt relieved and surprisingly sad. It almost looked as though he had given in to exhaustion.

"He's dead, isn't he?" my friend asked. Our guy grinned again and asked me to get him some tissue so he could take it outside. The guy who had just beaten a fierce competitor like that with crafty furniture moves, a can of Raid, and a flashlight didn't want to pick up a rat by the tail. Look, he had done it, and now he wanted tissue. I got some for him. He picked up the rat, went out the door, saying he'd be back in a minute to put the room back together for us. He came back in about twenty minutes, carrying a lot of fresh bedding and did the job. I gave him some cash; it couldn't be enough under the circumstances. He grinned again and, as he left, promised us some poison in the morning.

I slept fitfully that night. I had half-asleep visions of an army of rat cousins, uncles, aunts, etc. At one point when I did drift off, I dreamed that a huge battalion-sized single rat bigger than the whole resort came in and sat on the bed for a little chat. Thankfully I don't remember what he said.

My experiences with the rats, the two-legged kind, have happily been few and far between—actually about the same number of encounters as with the four-leggers.

The two-leggers don't skitter around and dive under your sofa or bed. They certainly won't take cheese from a trap, but only with wine and fancy crackers. Their characteristics are basically lying and cheating, but no matter how much you feel like it, you're not allowed to hit them on the head with a flashlight or squirt them with a can of Raid. Also, unlike the four-leggers, they can even have a certain charm. They'd have to, to get you to believe them in the first place. Unlike the four-leggers, they can make you laugh, enlighten you, and even make you feel you've found a new best friend.

And yet, while it is unlikely they will ever cause you to suddenly jump up on a sofa, they, too, can haunt your dreams.

On balance, and after careful consideration, I prefer the four-leggers.

I know only two tunes: One is "Yankee Doodle,"
and the other isn't.

—ULYSSES S. GRANT

Classical Music

LIKE ALMOST ANYONE IN the world, I love music. Unlike most people, I know anyway, I have a hard time with classical music. Well, "hard time" is a little bit of an understatement. I'll do anything to avoid hearing it. My only excuse is a childhood trauma, but I don't remember any. This has been so embarrassing that I've considered listening to classical under hypnosis, so I could sobbingly recall someone pulling my puppy's ears off. The problem is, I didn't have a puppy.

The only explanation I can come up with is whenever I heard classical music while growing up, it was during sad or stressful events. Funerals and graduations. So now, of course, when it comes on, I feel sad and tense.

While I was still a teenager, I told my cousin Elliot about this. Elliot was a jock, but he loved Sibelius, particularly *Finlandia*. He put it on and watched me carefully. I nodded appreciatively for the first thirty seconds or so with all the cymbals crashing and drums beating, but then inevitably grew sad and tense.

Over the years at small dinner gatherings the hostess will throw on some classical. I try to be polite, but after five minutes or so it's hard not to notice my head on the table, and my secret comes out. People try to persuade me differently for a few minutes, but my sorrow just deepens. After a quick change to Ella Fitzgerald, or anything, I am once more sitting erect and acting dinner party-like. I know people resent my controlling the music that way, but I can't help it.

Sometimes going to meetings on high floors in buildings in New York, I'm trapped with classical Muzak and arrive for my appointment needing a glass of water and some fresh air before I can proceed. My attorney's phone has classical music when his secretary puts me on hold. Since I'm never in that great a mood when I'm calling an attorney in the first place, that one is really a bummer.

I've gotten by with help from my friends on this one. When people know I'm coming, they have something else on—even Grand Ole Opry is OK—so the only place I can really still run into it is at a restaurant, where I sometimes don't pick it up immediately, with all the hubbub coming in, checking coats, and finding my table. Once seated and I hear it, rather than ask everyone to get up and leave, I tough it out. On those occasions the bar bill is higher than usual.

The most exhausting thing in life . . . is being in-sincere.

—ANNE MORROW LINDBERGH

Fake Voices

WHY DO STEWARDESSES OR people on recordings feel compelled to speak with fake voices?

I once had an attorney who spoke to me as though I were sitting in front of a stadium full of people. I turned around in his office to make sure I was alone.

On a recent flight the stewardess refreshingly described the dinner like a friendly aunt: "Don't forget to eat all those veggies that come with that yummy chicken." Her genuine warmth was a welcome contrast with all the fake warmth so many stewardesses had been shoveling out over the years. Maybe it's hard to be really warm as you endlessly fly over the country, but there must be something between the real thing and a robot.

Another annoying stewardess move is putting strange emphasis on her announcements: "The captain *has* turned on the seat belt sign." Strange emphasis with a fake voice—give us a break!

Who do the people on recorded messages think they're talking to? Other recorded messages? We seem to be surrounded by recorded messages. "If you want this, press one. If you want that, press two." And on and on and press and press. I'm still assuming these are people and not computers talking.

Let me put it this way: If there are any people out

there making these recordings, OK, let's forget about warmth, but if you can't sound at least a little real, don't talk to humans.

The best idea I've ever heard on the subject came from the great radio entertainer Arthur Godfrey. While he had millions of listeners, he spoke as though he were talking to one person and that person were a close friend. It really works.

The race is not always to the swift, nor the battle to the strong—but that's the way to bet it.

—DAMON RUNYON

Playing Sports

WHEN I WAS A boy, I played all available sports. I played softball, baseball, football, basketball, soccer, tennis, golf. I even boxed.

One day, while playing soccer in my backyard, another boy missed the ball and gave me a hard kick in my ten-year-old leg. That night, while examining a blue egg halfway between my ankle and my knee, I began to have second thoughts about soccer, meaning I decided to drop the sport.

I was enjoying remarkable success as a boxer at the local Y. I had won all my bouts. Then one day another boy hit me so hard in the head the ring posts seemed to jump in the air and twist around the way Baryshnikov did at the top of his game. Motivated by fear, I won that fight as well, but shortly thereafter I announced my retirement from that sport.

The first time a baseball missed my head by inches I became a spectator of the national pastime.

I always loved basketball. I loved the shooting, the passing, the running, the whole deal. I remember walking home from pickup games in the gym in high school, my hair still wet from the shower, freezing into ice. I even loved that. Then one day basketball became more about pushing, shoving, throwing elbows into the opposition's stomach and face. I took a seat in the stands and cheered the others on.

One day I tried out for a sandlot football team. I was required to stand at the bottom of a hill in T-shirt and jeans and tackle a fully equipped larger fellow who tore down a hill into me. He ran up my body over my face. I did tackle him, and I was invited to join the team. I declined.

Softball I held on to. Tennis I gave up because my older brother was a local champion, and who needs that? Golf was of the miniature variety, and that stayed, but overall, by twenty I was pretty much a spectator of sports.

I'm not really embarrassed by any of this. I actually get some satisfaction out of it. You'll never see me on crutches because of a ski accident.

The only physical jeopardy I put myself in today comes from certain unavoidable situations in the movies, and there, I assure you, I won't be riding horseback across the plains a la Kevin Costner.

Recently a friend of mine told me he and a group of his business associates were going to "shoot the rapids" in some river in Colorado. Having had some experience with rapids in the movies, I strongly advised him against it. "You are a husband and father," I argued. "You don't need any rapids shooting." He answered that such feats made him feel more alive than anything he could do *out* of the rapids. None of my well-reasoned points had any impact.

On returning from the trip a few weeks later, he said two of the boats had overturned, sending executives flying through the air upside down at terrifying speeds. While his boat had not turned over, witnessing it all caused him to announce the end of his career on the rapids.

For most of us, participating in sports—it's just a matter of time.

Now that she is dead, she greets Christ with a nod.

—VIRGINIA TAYLOR

Snobs and Bigots

LIVING IN THE PROTECTED environment I do, I seldom have the opportunity to run into snobs. I've only met three that I can recall at the moment. There may have been a lot more all over the place, but snobs, as a rule, pretty much try to keep their snobbery under cover, around me anyway.

Two of these three snobs I worked on movies with. Two different movies. A man and a woman. They both raised their eyebrow a lot. One, the man, dismissed the entire country we were working in on the drive from the airport into town. This guy later went on to a fine career in television—playing a snob.

The woman was worse. She never really said anything all that snobby. She just carefully selected whom she spoke to. I assume both of these people must have been fairly frightened and insecure. I'm sure that's true, but it didn't make it any easier to be around them.

The third snob I met was a famous fashion designer who always seemed to be in an attitude of total disdain for everyone and everything around him. *Both* his eyebrows were always way up there. Somehow I once got invited to a large party at his home. I'm not sure how this mistake was made, but I turned up in a light brown knit suit, and the other two hundred or so people were all in tuxes. It was a cheap brown suit from one of my movie wardrobes, and this guy probably could spot that about a hundred yards away. I was standing with a few people when he came by to say hello. He never even glanced at me. Happily a friend of mine who's even more out of it than I am turned up later wearing a sport jacket and no tie, relieving me of some pressure.

Bigots, on the other hand, seem to abound everywhere, and they assume everyone around them is also a bigot. I don't know what other explanation there is for all this antiblack, -Jew, -gay talk it's so easy to hear. When people deny America is a racist country, I'm shocked.

I've gotten into some rough ones with cabdrivers who try to tell me that being black in America is no different from what the Jews, Irish, Italians went through in getting established. C'mon!

A white writer once made himself up to look black and discovered all the discrimination that poured over him. He wrote a book called *Black Like Me*, which was later made into a movie. The only thing I find surprising about all of this is that there are still so many people who claim there's no significant antiblack feeling in America. If you're a white person who feels you're not a racist, would you as joyously welcome news that your son or daughter was marrying a black person as you would a white?

Growing up in America, it's hard to be color-blind.

Apologize: to lay the foundation for a future offense.

—AMBROSE BIERCE

Apologies

I'VE FOUND THAT APOLOGIES can cause a lot of trouble. Somebody does something to you—like maybe snaps at you in conversation. Then he says, "I'm sorry." You say, "OK, but it's really unpleasant to be snapped at." The first person snaps louder, "I *said* I was *sorry!*"

Often apologies open a door of discussion on why the person did the thing he had to apologize for. *That's* really loaded. That could end up with screaming and slamming of doors.

Then there's the "Y'know, if you wouldn't do this, then I wouldn't do that." That one is usually answered with "The reason I do that is because you did *that!*" *"That!"* the other person retorts. "I never did *that!*" It's a mess.

There are people who never apologize, just treat other people badly and send expensive gifts on holidays. That's a tough one because while no one wants to be treated badly, you can get some incredible gifts.

Then there's the apology that does more harm than good. "Honey, while you were away, I had an affair with that cute blonde who works in the drugstore. It's over now, and it was nothing more than a powerful sexual thing. I'm sorry."

Nobody ever seems to know what to do with the apology that's not accepted. There always seems to be a moment when the person doing the apologizing wonders if it's legal for it not to be accepted. I didn't accept an apology once and threw the other person into a state of total bafflement over what to do next. It got particularly confusing for him because I continued on (it was a work situation) as though everything were normal, but we both knew there was that unaccepted apology hanging over us.

The whole apology question is so inflammatory that I really go out of my way to behave so I don't have to give one and to try to be around people who act nice enough that they don't have to give one to me.

Of course, the only way to fully avoid all of this is to stay in your room and never speak, but then you'd end up having to apologize for that.

What's a thousand dollars? Mere chicken feed. A poultry matter.

—GEORGE S. KAUFMAN

Shopping

I GO SHOPPING ONLY when absolutely necessary. Fortunately just about all my clothes come from movies. I usually can buy my wardrobe for half price, or they'll give it
to me. It depends how they feel about me when the
movie's over.

The only thing I haven't had trouble buying in a
store is underwear and socks. I've been looking for a
chocolate brown cotton sweater for about six years. I've
never seen one. I have, on occasion, gone through large
stores and not been able to find one thing to buy. Almost
everything seems to have someone's name on it, or an
alligator or a penguin. My little boy's jacket has about six
things written on the back of it. It's a great jacket, but he
looks like a walking ad.

I deeply don't want to walk around with someone's
name on my shirt, not even my own. Let the designers
walk around with our names on their shirts! An inside
label—fine, but c'mon! And what's with the pictures of
animals on everything? I honestly don't get it. How
about just a nice shirt? No names, no animals.

I'm so out of it on this subject that for about ten
years I wore a size 15½ collar on a dress shirt. Amazing
as it may seem, I figured your neck size was like your
arm length. It was what it was. So for a decade in there,
when my neck went from 15½ to 17 without my realizing

247

it, every time I put on a tie I'd almost choke to death, and I've got a decent IQ, too. I still don't like the idea of ties, but during that decade I was astonished anyone would *ever* put one on. I take responsibility for that one.

In general salespeople make me nervous. I once tried to buy an apartment in New York. I had a broker who used the word "integrity" a lot. I said I wasn't interested in a terrace. She showed me an apartment with a terrace. I said I didn't want a terrace. She said the terrace (which surrounded half the apartment) belonged to another apartment. Integrity.

I bought an expensive car from an experienced car salesman who didn't know if it had an FM radio. It did. He then called me to see if I would read a book a friend of his wrote to help get it published. I don't think he believed me when I told him it had just taken me five years to get something of mine published. He then called again because he wanted to know, "How do you enjoy dealing with me?" After censoring a lot of stuff, I just said, "Fine."

I realize a lot of my problems with shopping are my own fault. Somehow I got it into my mind that if I bring a new shirt or hat into my house, it really becomes part of my life—like my inner circle. I mean, I don't have that much stuff, so I see these shirts and hats every day. They end up living in my private places—my closet, my shelf. I think of them more as new roommates, so I know I take it too seriously.

If it wasn't for getting most of my clothes from work, I'm sure I'd be a nervous wreck with only underwear, socks, two shirts, and a hat.

Infidel: in New York, one who does not believe in the Christian religion; in Constantinople, one who does.

—AMBROSE BIERCE

Xmas Trees

AS A BOY GROWING up in an Orthodox Jewish family, Christmas always made me uneasy. I knew it was to celebrate the birth of Christ, and I'd heard it around that the Jews killed Christ, even though when I saw the movie *The Robe,* it seemed the Romans did it. Nevertheless, in my area there wasn't any anti-Roman feeling, just anti-Semitic.

I never heard (if the Jews did kill Christ) why they killed him. I felt sure they certainly wouldn't have done it (if they did it) had they known he was the son of God.

When the Christmas trees all were lighted in the Christian homes, through the windows it looked like a warm, cozy setting with us killers on the outside.

This has been my feeling most of my life. A few years ago my Jewish wife suggested we get a tree. I was astonished at the idea and told her my reasons. She made a case that the tree wasn't what I said, but more a general celebration of a festive spirit—or something like that. We went back and forth on it for a while, and now, much to my amazement, we have a tree.

I intend to keep having them, partially in hope that the Christians will drop the killer thing and we all have a Christmas drink together.

A lot of fellows nowadays have a B.A., M.D., or Ph.D. Unfortunately, they don't have a J.O.B.

—FATS DOMINO

Jobs and Money (What Do People Want and Why?)

WHEN I WAS EIGHTEEN years old, I saw a movie starring Elizabeth Taylor and Montgomery Clift and decided I wanted to become a movie star. It had nothing to do with a job or money. It had to do with romance. I had a crush on Elizabeth Taylor. As for acting, it was a profession in which I had no experience except for my role of Don, the janitor boy, in *Getting Gracie Graduated*, my grammar school play, but part of Montgomery Clift's genius was he made acting look easy. After a short while I realized that acting was even harder than meeting Elizabeth Taylor.

At that point I forgot about being a movie star and even Elizabeth Taylor and became fascinated with learning about the craft of acting. Still, none of this in any way felt like a job, and the subject of money to me was where did I get ten dollars a week to pay my rent.

I got my money with part-time jobs that paid for rent and acting classes. That was it. I wasn't even thinking about making a lot of money or being famous. I was only thinking about getting better at acting.

As time went by and I began to work as an actor, make money, and even achieve some fame, I still basically thought about the work, not the money or fame. As I've said, I stayed in my small apartment in New York with no stove.

It seems that then, as now, professionally I defined a work experience more by what was it like to be there than how successful it turned out. The quality of life was what it's been about. Some people that I've met and befriended for a time haven't seen it that way. They are what I think of as the careerists. Success and fame seem to outstrip all other considerations, such as human relationships. I'm sure, of course, these people inhabit every profession. The work, they tell themselves, is the thing. Everything comes after the work—friendships, family, whatever. These people even seem to take a sense of professional pride in this attitude, as though it made them a little more dedicated than their co-workers. To me it shows a desperation and an inability to sustain much interest for any period of time in anything beyond their personal advancement. These people can be bright, charming, and may even appear to be interested in you—but not really, unless you can help their careers.

They may say they do all this for their families, but their families usually just want them, not more money. Careerists bore easily if you're not talking about them or their field, and they can make you feel boring. These people can definitely be damaging to your health.

What do they want? One former friend seems to want to be the richest person in the world. A friend of mine once said that all these money seekers should get together and live above a bank. Most of these people have no strong friendships. I remember seeing Lena Horne once on *60 Minutes* announce ruefully something to the effect of "I've had a hell of a career, but I don't have any friends."

I don't believe we choose to be the way we are in

this area. As I've said, friends have always been a necessity to me. My life needs that. I can't sit in a nice home, have a good bank account, and feel warm all over. I require the love of family and friends. If offered a choice, I'll take less money and more friends. I'm grateful I'm that way, just as I'm sorry I'm some other ways.

I guess the best we can do for ourselves in this or any department is try to figure out what we really think and feel and are we happy with it. If we can answer that question, maybe what follows helps us get through life a little bit better.

Nothing helps scenery like ham and eggs.

—MARK TWAIN

Sometimes We're Just Hungry

WHEN MY DAUGHTER, MARION, was a young teenager, she came to visit me on the set of a movie I was doing with Jeff Bridges. At the end of the day, as we drove home together, she seemed very withdrawn.

"What's the matter?" I asked her.

"Nothing," she said too quickly.

"Come on," I said, "it's obvious something is wrong."

"No, nothing," she again said quickly.

"Marion," I said, "I can feel it. You're never this quiet. What is it?"

"What do you mean, I'm never this quiet? What kind of a thing is that to say to me?"

"I don't mean any offense, honey," I said. "I just mean I know you, and this isn't you. What is it?"

"You *think* you know me. You'd be very surprised!" she snapped.

"Well, surprise me," I said. "I like surprises."

"This isn't funny!" she said.

"I didn't say it was funny. I'm just asking you what's going on."

There was a long silence as I continued our drive home. Finally she said, "Jeff Bridges doesn't know I'm alive."

"What?" I asked.

"Jeff Bridges," she repeated, "he doesn't know I exist."

"Uh-huh," I said cautiously.

"What's that mean?" she quickly asked.

"No, nothing," I carefully said. "I just meant I heard you."

"How old is he anyway?" she asked.

"Oh, I don't know, twenty-eight or so."

"Mmm," she said, "I thought more like twenty-three."

"No, I think more like twenty-eight." We continued to drive in silence. Finally I said, "I'll tell you the truth, Marion. I don't actually think you are upset about Jeff Bridges. I think you're just hungry."

Marion exploded on that one. "I hate it when you do that," she said. "You always try to joke me out of everything. I hate it!"

I foolishly persisted. "Well, just tell me when did you last have something to eat?"

"Stop it, Daddy!" she shouted at me. "Just stop it!"

"OK," I said. "I wasn't trying to joke you out of anything. I've just noticed that sometimes you get to feeling a little down when you haven't eaten."

"Daddy!" she yelled.

"OK," I said. We drove in silence for another minute. I began to talk about the movie in general, but Marion wasn't very responsive.

As we finally pulled into the driveway, she said, "I just think he's a very cute guy."

I said, "He is, honey, but you don't even know him, and he is a little old for you."

"Yeah," she said disconsolately as we went into the house.

Inside Marion walked into the living room, flipped on the television set, and stared at it vacantly. I threw together some cheeseburgers; we sat in front of the television set and ate them. The cheeseburgers and the show came to an end at the same time, and Marion leaped to her feet and told me a hilarious story about going shopping with her grandmother and how her grandmother was just the last person to try to push around, as more than one salesperson had discovered. Marion acted out the parts of her grandmother and the salesmen brilliantly, and we both were laughing uncontrollably when she finished.

Gasping for breath, I said, "Hey, Marion, I thought you were upset about Jeff Bridges."

Marion stopped and thought a moment. "Jeff Bridges?" she said. "I don't care about Jeff Bridges. I don't even know him."

I stared at her.

"Hey," she said, "maybe I *was* just hungry."

To his physician, who said, "General, I fear the angels are waiting for you." "Waiting, are they? Waiting, are they? Well . . . let 'em wait!"

—ETHAN ALLEN

Don't Get Too Excited

I'M WRITING THIS PIECE on the MGM Grand Airline. I'm flying from Los Angeles to New York. I'm in first class in the most luxurious airplane I've ever been on. My champagne glass is constantly refilled. There's caviar and sturgeon sitting on plates around the champagne. This is all being paid for by Universal Pictures, MCA, which has recently been bought by the Japanese. The Japanese are getting me high. They're doing all this because I've just returned from meeting the people who are making the next movie I get to star in. It's written by John Hughes, who last wrote *Home Alone,* and produced by Ivan Reitman, who, among many other successes, produced and directed *Ghostbusters.* Also, I get paid a lot of money. It's a good life, except yesterday my cousin Paul died. I loved my cousin Paul. He married my cousin Phyllis, who is my mother's sister's daughter. My mother's sister died in her late twenties from a mastoid condition—an ear problem easily curable today. Phyllis was always my prototype of the woman I was looking for—warm and nice to look at. She married Paul, who was also warm—and shy. He was a successful optometrist. R. Paul Zusman was his name. I don't know what the R. was for. I just know he was one of the nicest guys I ever met in my life. It's not a long list either. I mean, people who are always, always, consistently nice over a lifetime.

267

Paul was very athletic. He played a lot of sports—full out. He was in great shape. He sometimes had some back problems but not enough to keep him from playing squash full out at seventy, which he was doing five minutes before he fainted. He went so fast he didn't even have time to touch his heart. No knowledge of a prior heart condition—just extending himself too much, I guess. That's why regular stress tests are important. Who knows? Last week it was my friend Danny Thomas. He went almost as fast as Paul. Danny hadn't exercised. What they had in common prior to dying was they had pushed themselves. Danny had just come back from an extensive book tour. He had signed eight hundred books on the last day of his tour. That means talking to eight hundred people. I'm considerably younger than both these men, and I couldn't play squash full out for very long or sign books and talk to fifty people in a day.

It's dark outside the plane window somewhere over mid-America, and while I should feel excited about my good fortune, I can only think about my friends now gone. Champagne does that, I guess, but then I felt all this before I got on the plane.

I try never to get too excited.

We know what happens to people who stay in the middle of the road. They get run over.

—ANEURIN BEVAN

Politics

I THINK THE REASON Ronald Reagan's opponents always underestimated him is that they just thought he was a bad movie actor.

Ronald Reagan starred in about fifty-five movies. You don't star in fifty-five movies for no reason at all. You sure don't star in them if you're just a bad actor.

Ronald Reagan starred in all those movies because he was enormously appealing and likable. With rare exceptions, we always elect the more appealing of the two guys President. It's not what they say; it's who do we want to look at for the next four years.

The two exceptions to this case in modern times came with Barry Goldwater and George McGovern. For me, Barry Goldwater was much more appealing than Lyndon Johnson, and George McGovern much more appealing than Richard Nixon, but they both lost. A lot of people felt Goldwater, if elected, would blow up the world and that McGovern was some kind of a leftist, hippie socialist/Communist. In my opinion, Goldwater wouldn't have, and McGovern wasn't, but they had each said enough peculiar things that the unappealing guys won.

George Bush, who seemed like he could be the appealing star of a TV series, *Love That George*, ran against Michael Dukakis, who always looked like he had a headache. Of course, Bush won.

I was a writer for Dukakis in his presidential campaign. I got a call from someone asking me to appear
with the governor in a rally in a small town outside Pittsburgh. That call was my first indication that people in
charge of this campaign didn't quite know what they
were doing. Having me appear at a rally for Governor
Dukakis outside Pittsburgh isn't worth the plane fare
they paid or even the cab fare to the airport. It just
doesn't matter. I don't believe it matters about any celebrities appearing (Redford appeared for Dukakis, too); I
mean, does anyone care, when voting for President,
which celebrities are for him?

I flew to the rally. I even spoke. The people looked
quizzical, like "I know that face from somewhere." There
was no surge in the polls. Jennifer Beals from the movie
Flashdance was with me. I think they shot some of that
movie in Pennsylvania. That's why she was there. She
was very nice. She didn't speak. She waved. Afterward
Sam Donaldson and his crew almost knocked me down
as he ran toward Jennifer, thrust a microphone in her
face, and said, "I understand you're from Pittsburgh."
She stared a moment and said, "No." He stared back,
then ran down the street after someone else.

I actually flew to this thing because I was told I'd
have a chance to speak to Dukakis. I had earlier learned
that he had no media adviser—no Roger Ailes, anyway,
on his campaign. I believe, as strange as it seems, there
was a relationship between what I had been doing for
twenty years on *The Tonight Show* and what he needed to
think about, which is communicating in a brief
way—sound bites, they call them. I also wanted to ask
why he felt it wasn't necessary to answer all the attacks
on him. I had heard he felt it was demeaning to respond
to the ads that clearly implied if he were President, all
the murderers would be turned free and all the water-

ways would be floating garbage dumps. He assumed, I had heard, everyone knew better, even though he was losing support at an alarming pace. His cousin Olympia Dukakis later told me, "Michael's not the kind of person who gets into the trenches and fights like that." He's more an above-the-fray statesman type of guy. (Not a bad tactic if you're already President.)

I finally did get to meet with Dukakis in a room at the airport. He was sitting there with his daughter. He thanked me for coming. I asked how he felt, and he said he felt more comfortable during the primary, which featured more hour-long debates. He said now you had to think more in short sound bites, and he wasn't inclined that way. It was a perfect opportunity for me to stress the importance of becoming inclined that way, but as I was about to speak, he said, "Do you know John?" I had no idea who he meant. I said, "John?" He said, "John Dukakis. *He's* an actor." The question felt to me like asking someone from Italy if he knows another person from Italy. I mean, as hard as it may be to believe, Katharine Hepburn met Henry Fonda for the first time in the movie *On Golden Pond.* Anyway, I never got to say anything more to the governor as he was called away, but I did speak to someone else who welcomed me aboard to help any way I could. I threw a couple things to headquarters in the vein of Reagan to Carter—"There you go again"—or Bentsen to Quayle—"You're no Jack Kennedy." I think my best suggestion was he look at Bush at some point in a debate after a Bush answer, take a long pause, and say, "You've got to be kidding," or "Aw, c'mon!" but I've never heard him say anything like that. They wanted celebrities with them but didn't have any idea how to use anyone. Norman Lear gave a big gathering at his home. The room was packed with a lot of people who had risen to the top of show business.

Dukakis could have learned a lot from these people, or people who had risen to the top of any profession. He never really asked anything. I think most people went home feeling like I did, deciding to mind their own business again. It's an easy cop-out I'm not proud of.

Why do people go into politics anyway? I'm sure a decent percentage of them really want to help people. Unfortunately it feels like a bigger percentage of them just want to be center stage. After all, a lot of actors go into politics after they're not particularly in demand in show business, and a surprising number of politicians were frustrated in artistic pursuits. Just think, if Hitler had made it as a painter (and he wasn't a bad one from stuff I've seen) . . .

The whole idea of helping people, whether it's politics or doctors or lawyers or whatever, seems to get lost along the way so often—lost to the demands of the ego. Ironically the people who really are there primarily to help others will tell you it's the best possible way to *have* a healthy ego.

In any case, being in show business all my life, I probably look at politicians a little differently. I'm always trying to spot one who doesn't seem like he wants to get into my profession. Sadly I don't have a long list.

Winter lingered so long in the lap of Spring that it occasioned a great deal of talk.

—BILL NYE

Weather

MY DOMINANT FOCUS ON weather has to do with avoiding getting sick.

So if it's a hot, sunny day, when most people think of going to the beach, I think of not going from heat to air conditioning. On cold, snowy days, when some people think of skiing, I think of thermal underwear.

In Los Angeles I've noticed there doesn't seem to be such a thing as too hot. The weatherman will say, "Another gorgeous day, ninety-eight degrees." To me that's a hellhole.

When I was a little boy growing up in the cold winters of Pittsburgh, weather really had to do with survival. Often when I stepped off my front porch to go to school after a snowfall, I would disappear. Somebody bigger would have to pull me up by my head.

The most annoying thing to me about the weather is the weather report on TV. All most of us really want to know is what's the weather. They will show you patterns forming up here, down there, out over the ocean. For our actual weather we have to wait until after a commercial. Also, I'm a bit disturbed how these weather people and the anchorpeople they chat with act like it's up to the weatherman to decide what kind of weather we're going to get. "What have you got for us today?" they're asked. "Oh, I think maybe you're going to be happy."

Suddenly I feel like a five-year-old being teased—something we all hated even at five. And has anyone ever laughed at the weatherman's jokes besides his colleagues in the studio? I don't think so.

I can actually get nostalgic about the weather. I miss the winter clothes of childhood—leggings and knickers, mackinaws and earmuffs.

Finally, I think as you get older, dealing with weather (bad, at least) becomes a challenge to avoid. Time changes our attitude toward weather, along with everything else.

Advertising may be described as the science of arresting the human intelligence long enough to get money from it.

—STEPHEN LEACOCK

Advertising

WHEN I WAS A little boy, I thought that if any advertisement was printed in the paper or spoken on the radio, or later on television, it was true. There was a time I actually thought people *would* walk a mile for a Camel cigarette. I thought there really *was* such a thing as whiter than white, cleaner than clean. Now, of course, I realize it's all lies.

Even the makers of products that are good for you find it necessary to lie. This car, that perfume, or that beer really won't change your life; we all know that. A lot of us knew that if Dukakis had been elected President, all the murderers wouldn't go free the next day, and yet all these lies are allowed to go out over the airwaves constantly. These are the same airwaves where not too long ago you couldn't say the word "breast" or "thigh." I don't get it. What are the rules?

You could clearly suggest, as Lyndon Johnson's commercial did, that if Barry Goldwater were elected President, he'd blow up the world, but as I understand it, you couldn't mention Barry's thighs.

Most of the people who participate in all of this don't see it that way. People running the tobacco companies still go on television and say there's no real proof cigarettes are damaging to your health. We sell millions of tons of cigarettes now to foreign countries that don't know that much about cigarettes and cancer.

I sat next to an executive of a tobacco company on a long flight once. We had a nice talk until I expressed surprise he was smoking. He muttered a few things I couldn't quite follow, and we mutually retreated to our reading matter.

On the other hand, anyone who buys a car because a pretty girl is leaning on it probably deserves what he gets.

These, having not the law, are a law unto themselves.

—ROMANS 2:14

Cable TV Companies

HAVE CABLE TV COMPANIES been put on this earth to torture us or what? I'm not talking about cable TV itself, which I love. I'm talking about those wackos who control our getting our cable TV. Of course, not everyone who runs or works for a cable TV company is a wacko, but I do get the feeling the percentage runs a little higher there than throughout the land in general.

First of all, in New York anyway, it seems like most of the people can't even get cable TV. Years ago it was revealed that politicians in different boroughs of New York City wanted bribes, so to this day millions of concerned citizens usually can't get to see their sports teams. That deprivation, added to the other countless assaults that come with living in a big city, makes me want to kill the cable company operators and, of course, those wonderful public servants who wanted the bribes.

I have not personally suffered from this, as I have cable. My outrage is felt on behalf of my fellow sports fans and also because of my dealings with the cable companies. First of all, they regularly make appointments eight to one or one to six they don't keep! They just don't show up! They don't show up, and they don't call! You stay home and wait all day and keep hoping that door buzzer is them, but it isn't. Then, when you call to find out what happened, they put you on hold so long you could have a birthday.

Recently I ordered everything they've got. My new additions—Bravo, the Disney channel, and Showtime—were most welcome, except I don't get them. They're working on the problem, God help me.

Also, I've been trying to get rid of the sex channels for months now. They come in loud and clear. They asked me, "Are there children in the house?" "Yes," I said, "but there are even adults that don't want to look at this, believe it or not." I mean you can be flipping channels, even quickly, and you can't believe between an English movie and a weather report what will pop on in a big close-up.

All in all, I'm glad we have cable. I just think we should all be on notice that when we need service or anything else from the companies, we are entering the great unknown.

The roulette table pays nobody except him who keeps it. Nevertheless, a passion for gaming is common, though a passion for keeping roulette wheels is unknown.

—George Bernard Shaw

Gambling

I DIDN'T REALIZE I had a gambling problem until the first time I gambled and couldn't stop. It was at a dog track in Florida. I was a student at the University of Miami, and I split my time between the classes and the dogs. At Christmas break I was $135 in debt. In my life in the mid-1950s that was a fortune. I told my mother what had happened, asked for the money, and promised I wouldn't ever go back to the dogs. She gave it to me, and I kept the promise.

Over the years, though, I've been aware of the problem. There's a unique feeling of intoxication that all gamblers must know. I guess when you've worked for a dollar an hour and less in your life, as most of us have, and with a flip of a card, etc., you can make a hundred dollars, that's a heady feeling. Of course, there's the opposite as well.

Recently, when working on a movie, I had to go to Las Vegas. I had avoided this my whole life. I knew I would be drawn to the tables. I quickly walked through the casino in the lobby of the hotel where I was staying. When I got to my room, I called my wife as though I were a recovering alcoholic staring at a bottle of vodka on a table.

Since my need to keep promises is greater than my need to gamble, I promised my wife I would quit after I lost one thousand dollars. I got the OK and flew to the tables. I quickly *won* a thousand dollars. I wasn't working that evening in the movie, but the company was. I walked around and showed all my pals my roll, as though I were a kid who somehow found a treasure chest of candy. A day later, of course, I had lost the thousand I'd won and the thousand I was allowed to lose.

Now I had to keep my promise and stay away from the tables. The problem was we had a few more days' filming there. Happily I was working, but the gambling goes on twenty-four hours a day, so no matter when I finished work, 2:00 A.M., 3:00 A.M., I had to walk through the lobby with all that action around me. I stared straight ahead, concentrating on my promise till I made it into the elevator.

If I was a guy who broke promises, I probably couldn't afford the paper I'm writing this piece on.

Our life is frittered away by detail. . . . Simplify, simplify.

—Henry David Thoreau

The Ability to Feel

PEOPLE SEEM TO MEASURE the success of their life by the money they've earned, the positions they've reached. Some people might say if they've been married to the same person for forty-five years and raised two wonderful children, that's life's greatest achievement. Others might say a lot of people married forty five years have just been afraid to get a divorce, and everyone—for the record—says he has wonderful children. Actually, if all the children who have publicly been called wonderful were so wonderful, the world would have to be a better place, so personally I question all this wonderfulness.

For a long time I have felt the measure of a life's success has a lot to do with the ability to feel.

For a lot of people, including me, that's a tougher one than making money. I remember years ago a friend dragging me out of the house into a car and racing down a highway to get a particularly good angle on a sunset. My friend was bursting with excitement. I could see it was beautiful, but honestly no thrill was racing through my system. Later, when I had to go to Rome, I took my friend's parents with us. People said I was so generous. The truth was I knew I would be unmoved by Rome, but I would be moved by my friend's parents' response to it.

The ability to feel can be a tough one to those of us who have closed down out of a need to protect after experiencing some of life's blows. Finding that place be-tween an open wound and a detached personality isn't always so easy.

I've known people who others see as sitting on top of the world, because of their fame and fortune, who are able to feel nothing but fear and anxiety. How successful are they? Then, of course, there are those who society would view as failures who seem to experience all of life: the downs, yes, but also the sunrise, the sunset, a cool breeze, a warm breeze, everything—including love.

I think we need to rate the ability to feel somewhere above fame and fortune.

New York: No other city in the United States can divest the visitor of so much money with so little enthusiasm. In Dallas, they take it away with gusto; in New Orleans, with a bow; in San Francisco, with a wink and a grin. In New York, you're lucky if you get a grunt.

—FLETCHER KNEBEL

New York vs. Los Angeles

SHOW BUSINESS IN AMERICA is basically located in two cities, New York and Los Angeles, and show people are always debating which city is best.

The New Yorkers point out that there are no seasons in Los Angeles. The Los Angeles people say, "Who needs freezing winters or seasons of any kind?" The Los Angeles people love year-round sunshine and, it seems, the hotter, the better. On the other hand, there are certain freezing winter days in New York when L.A. does look pretty good. The real reason I have to give the nod to New York is that we don't have that unique-to-Los Angeles infamous "smog alert."

I'm a pretty literal guy, and when more often than you could imagine the radio announcer tells you, "Do not come out of your house today unless it's absolutely necessary," it does give me pause.

I was once doing a movie at Universal Studios, and because I was familiar with all these "Don't leave the house" warnings from earlier trips, I got a room at the Sheraton Universal next to the studio. I had to come out of the hotel every day, so I figured I'd keep my outdoors time down to a minimum.

On these smog alert days I would come dashing out the front door of the hotel, with a handkerchief over my face, and run about fifty yards as fast as I could to my

car in the parking lot. By the time I got in the car, my
eyes were watering and my stomach was upset because
my body is just not set up to start the day with a fifty-
yard dash. I would then drive less than five minutes to
the studio, park my car, and run again as fast as I could
to the makeup room. By the time I got there, my stomach
was really upset from my second dash, my eyes were
burning more, and a headache was beginning.

After the makeup I would once more dash back to
my dressing room, where I would have to lie down, eyes
watery, stomach upset, splitting headache. I also found
on these smog-warning days, when I didn't have to work
and would stay inside, I would still get the burning eyes
and the headache—I guess from air that just gets inside
your room somehow. The symptoms weren't as severe,
but all in all, I'll take the seasons in New York, even with
the freezing winters.

The other argument you hear against the Los
Angeles show business community is that there are a lot
of phonies and liars out there. Well, that always seemed
to me to be a pretty rough judgment to lay on a community, especially when the community laying it has its own
fair amount of phonies and liars. I'd have to say there
really is more of this kind of stuff in L.A., but then there
are more people in L.A. who are in show business.

I guess what bothers me the most about L.A. is that
people's response to you does seem to reflect to a tremendous degree how high up or down you happen to
be in the business that week. People there read the daily
trade papers more than they read the newspapers, it
seems, so they really keep track of who's hot and who's
not.

The advantage of being a New Yorker is, compara-
tively speaking, you really don't know what the hell is
going on as much in show business, life not being cen-

tered as much on these trade papers—or, as someone once referred to them, these score cards. Show business New Yorkers seem to have to spend a certain amount of energy just being able to function in New York at all. They don't seem to have the time or inclination to study trade papers on a daily basis; therefore, you're more likely to get more equal treatment in New York.

So I'd say, I'll take New York, based on ability to breathe, and ignorance.

The prince of darkness is a gentleman.

—WILLIAM SHAKESPEARE

The Dangers of Detachment

I SAW SOME SUNDAY morning commentators on television today discussing a Democratic politician's comments on the war in the gulf. The Democrat had said he'd rather see the war go well (if wars can go well) and lose the White House in '92 than have the war go badly and the Democrats win the White House. The commentators all chuckled, saying, "What do you expect a Democrat to say?" Clearly they didn't believe him, and just as clearly the commentators implied that if they were politicians of the opposing party saying that, they shouldn't be believed either. It was all like idle cocktail party chatter except it was about young people's lives. What was the truth? That any politician of an opposing party would understandably have to hope the war went badly so he could win office? Really? He would hope for more young people to die, so he could get elected? That was clearly the implication. If there's any truth to that, and I fear there is, then that's a danger of detachment.

I believed those commentators could feel more upset from their own headaches or sore toes than the abstract idea of a young person losing his life. It's a disease, this detachment. Most of the prison population suffered from it before they did their crimes. Someone steals two dollars and spends years of his life locked up. You have to have considerable detachment to not realize the possible

303

consequence of the crime. That's why I believe so much of the prison population is in a state of shock at being there—at first anyway.

I know I suffered from an acute sense of detachment when, at eighteen, I would swim in the ocean at night, and not close to shore either. I had just lost my dad. It's certainly not unusual that detachment goes hand in hand with self-destructiveness.

I think we all have to check our levels from time to time.

When I feel like exercising I just lie down until the feeling goes away.

—ROBERT M. HUTCHINS

Exercise

AT A CERTAIN POINT in everyone's life, exercise becomes an issue. It's certainly not there in childhood, although I hear they now have exercise classes for children—of rich families, I assume.

One summer evening I was walking into a restaurant with a friend of mine, and I noticed that his chest seemed to be fairly bursting through his shirt.

He told me that he'd met a man at the gym who was a workout expert, and this fellow was now coming to his house.

Two days later he showed up at my apartment, an imposing drill sergeant type of guy. I shook his hand and said how impressed I'd been with what he'd done with my friend. He nodded and said, "Let's go to work." He instantly launched me into sit-ups, push-ups, jumping up and down, bending side to side, bending back and forth. After about ten minutes of this I gasped that I hadn't really done anything like this for twenty years, if then. He nodded and said, "Keep working." He ordered me to pull my left leg forward to my chest twenty times, right leg, both legs, more sit-ups, push-ups. It had been about thirty minutes. I wanted to stop, but a deeply bred work ethic kept me gasping and obeying his commands. Finally, after a couple of more minutes, I said again that this felt like a little more than I could manage at the moment. He said, "Take a thirty-second break." I gratefully stopped and caught my breath. In thirty seconds he resumed with more of the same. As I wrenched my body into places it hadn't been for years, I tried jokes to slow him down. "Hey," I gasped, "I'm not going for the Olympics, you know." He stared, but as I stopped to get a chuckle break, he said, "Keep working." After fifty minutes of torment he said, "OK, that's it." Sweat was pouring out of me; I was completely "gone."

"All right, let's do ten minutes on the bike."

"What?" I said.

"Didn't you say you had an Exercycle?"

I did have an Exercycle I'd bought years ago that had pretty much become a conversation piece. After five minutes on the bike I thought no part of my body would ever move again. After ten minutes, he said, "OK, that's it. Just rest a few minutes and then have your shower." He said, "Good-bye," saying he'd see me again in three days, and pretty much marched out the door.

One hour later I hadn't moved. Later that day I got up and took a shower. That evening I called my friend and said the whole thing seemed to extend me more than I had in mind. He acknowledged that the guy was a pretty stern taskmaster and reminded me I was in charge and it was up to me to set the limits. I said, "How would you really know where your limit was?"

He said, "If you faint, you probably passed it."

The next session was a duplicate of the first.

I spoke to my friend again, saying that after only two sessions with the guy I was having nightmares about him standing in my doorway. "You're in charge," my friend repeated.

The third time he showed up, rather than direct confrontation, I tried the old third-person technique on him.

"I was telling my friend," I said, "that I actually have gotten to the point where I dread seeing you because this all feels like it's extending me too much."

He nodded and said, "Down on the floor."

Still driven by the instructor's iron will and my own willingness to push myself, three more similar sessions followed. Between sessions I started to just kind of lie around, trying to find a position where a particularly painful ache at the base of my spine might be accommodated. Not being able to find that position, and spending more and more time in bed, I phoned the instructor and reported my condition.

"You've probably been going at it a little too hard," he said.

"That's what I think," I said. "Why don't I give you a call when I feel up to it? [thinking, 'How about never?']."

"No," he quickly said, "we don't want to lose what we've already gained. We'll keep our regular session, but we'll just 'tone' you."

Amazingly I still assumed he must know more than I, so I reluctantly agreed.

After two toning sessions I was totally bedridden. In my next call to the instructor I asked if he could recommend a doctor.

He made another try at a toning session but backed off when I said my total activity these days was limping from the bed to the bathroom and back. He then recommended a doctor and wished me luck.

I hung up the phone and vowed that after having my back examined, I'd have my head examined.

I painfully limped to the doctor the drill sergeant had recommended, and after checking to see how far I could bend over (which was not at all) and then checking out

my other physical capabilities (which were nothing to
write home about either), he suggested I immediately be
put into the hospital.

He said I needed to lie flat on my back for two
weeks, and somehow two vertebrae that were squeezing
a disk would lay off. He called it sciatica. In the past,
whenever my back was giving me any trouble (and that
trouble was like a party compared with this), people
would ask if I had sciatica, and I always recoiled in horror
and said, "Oh, no!" Sciatica, to me, always sounded like
rabies. I didn't even want to know what it was, and now
I had it. Still, going to the hospital for two weeks seemed
a little extreme to me, so I said, "How about I do all this
bed rest at home?" He said that was fine, but that in his
experience people didn't really do it at home, and he
thought the hospital was the ticket. I assured him I'd do
it right at home, thanked him, and left.

At home, over the next two weeks, I turned out to be
just like everyone else. I lay there awhile; I got restless; I
walked around; I got worse.

I started limping around town to other doctors. I
went to a chiropractor and was helped for a few hours.
I got shots of different kinds and was helped for a day
or so. I even went to a doctor on Park Avenue who stuck
a needle up each nostril and kept them there for twenty
minutes: nothing. I got a prescription for Percodan, a
very strong pain-killer, and even though soon I could
barely move at all, I was pretty happy about everything
anyway, because of the euphoric element of the drug.
Finally a day came when I had an appointment with a
particularly highly recommended orthopedic man, and I
absolutely couldn't get there. Since I was now crawling
to and from the bathroom, I began to think the first doctor was right, and I should be put into the hospital. I
called the new doctor's office and said I'd be unable to

keep my appointment as I couldn't move. The secretary was really miffed at me for not showing up. I said, "Couldn't the doctor arrange to have me put in the hospital?"

She said, "The doctor won't put anyone in the hospital he hasn't seen. Why don't you call an ambulance and keep your appointment so the doctor can see you?"

I said, "You mean, be wheeled through your waiting room on a stretcher to see if I qualify for the hospital?"

She said, "That's right, if that's the only way the doctor can see you."

The thought of the doctor coming to see me at home never entered her mind or, for that matter, mine, being properly conditioned by modern times. I thanked her, told her I thought I'd explore other possibilities, and said good-bye. She said good-bye as though I had deeply insulted her and the doctor by not having myself wheeled in.

I got the name of another doctor, who, on hearing my story on the phone, arranged to have me put in the hospital. By that time I was taking massive amounts of pain-killers, having no idea they were addictive. The ambulance came; I was wheeled through the lobby of my building, with a lot of elderly people staring at me and shaking their heads sadly. I was admitted to the hospital after lying on the stretcher in the lobby for a long time and answering every question modern man can think of to ask. Even here my mother's maiden name seemed of crucial importance.

Shortly after I was put in my room, the doctor arrived with a young associate. Since it was a teaching hospital, he immediately asked me to get out of bed and walk across the room to see the degree of my problem. I got up out of the bed, took one step, and immediately fell to the floor. The doctor looked at his associate and said, "Now that's a severe injury." I lay on the floor and looked at them as they nodded in mutual understanding. A nurse helped me back into bed. The doctor said, "You'll need an operation. We'll schedule a myelogram to see exactly where the damage is, and I'll see you soon."

Over the past few weeks I had heard about these myelograms. Evidently they injected a dye into your spine, and then an X ray told them exactly where the trouble was. I also had heard that sometimes these myelograms could give you a headache that could last for twenty-five years or as long as you lived, whichever was longer—in other words, forever. I had also heard that in recent years they had found a way to do it without the headache part, but I still wasn't so anxious to sign up.

The next morning four people in white uniforms came into my room and started to wheel me out the door. I was pretty strongly drugged with my Percodan. I looked up and asked what the deal was. They said they had a sudden opening for a myelogram and, since they were so hard to get, slid me right in the slot. Remembering the twenty-five-year-headache possibility, I said, "Hold it! I haven't agreed to any myelogram." They said the doctor felt I needed one. "Not necessarily," I said quickly, as they slowly came to a halt in their wheeling. "I'd like the doctor to check me again before we go in this direction." They said the myelogram openings were pretty rare. "I'll take my chances," I said. They turned me around and wheeled me back into my room.

The next day the doctor told me it was fine with him to see what would happen if I lay flat out for the next three weeks. He said if I took just one step, it would undo a full day's recuperation. I would now have to become a bedpan fella. He also said it was time to start coming off the Percodan.

After coming off Percodan for eight days of my three-week stay, I became convinced that my recovery would be greatly aided if I could just get out of that hospital. I explained I had a running battle with the night nurse about having visitors after seven o'clock, which is about the only time my friends were free to come. I found I was the kind of person who liked a friend or two around while I withdrew from drugs. If you normally feel sad ten times a day—on drug withdrawal you're sobbing ten times a day. The nurse told me if I didn't like the 7 P.M. rule, I could speak to her supervisor. I did, and it turned out that her supervisor knew me from the movies, and now I had not a 7 P.M. curfew but an 11 P.M. and an enemy for a nurse. No amount humor on my part could dent her anger. "I can't have an enemy give me an enema," I cracked. She glared.

I also had a little trouble with their policy of coming into the room at 6:00 A.M. to see if you were still there, in more ways than one. I explained that the only way I wasn't going to be there was if I walked out in the night, and since I hadn't been able to take a step for months, it was highly unlikely that I'd be a runaway. After telling the doctor I felt I could be more relaxed doing the whole flat-on-my-back thing at home, and I had three friends who would stay with me on eight-hour shifts for the twenty-four-hour day, he agreed reluctantly to let me go.

And so eight days into my three-week stay, they wheeled me out as they had wheeled me in. They put me in an ambulance to take me home. I had a close friend riding shotgun with me in the ambulance, and that was lucky because the fellow riding in the back with us was given to a lot of dropping-guys-off-stretchers humor. He didn't know I was withdrawing from drugs and a little on the edgy side without those jokes. My pal got him to lay off all that, and he began to tell us all the designations for what they ran into in the ambulance field. DOA we already knew was "dead on arrival"; LOB was "liquor on breath," which wasn't hard to guess; but LRG/DNR we had no idea was "last rites given/do not resuscitate." In any case, I couldn't wait to get the hell away from him. They carried me back through the lobby of my building—the old people there shook their heads more sadly than before—and soon I was back in my own bed, flat out, with around-the-clock friends.

After a couple of weeks the doctor came to my apartment, breaking all modern medical tradition. Here was my moment of truth. He said if I couldn't stand up now, I'd need that operation after all. I hadn't stood for months, and the last time I tried I fell down. I was very nervous as I stood. I didn't fall. I didn't take a brisk walk, but I didn't fall. Barely. Slowly but surely, over a period of weeks, I came back to full strength. The doctor put me on a regimen of exercise to build up back muscles that I have followed religiously to this day, ten years later. The exercises not only give you strong back muscles, but as a side effect you start to have a really developed upper body. I now look pretty much like my friend.

There had to be an easier way.

I must get out of these wet clothes and into a dry martini.

—ROBERT BENCHLEY

Drinking

WHEN I WAS GROWING up, there was always a bottle of whiskey in the dining-room cabinet. It took about fifteen years to drink it. This happened incrementally during religious events or possibly one or two celebratory occasions over the years. No one in the house drank. No one who visited the house drank. This was a house occupied by Jewish people primarily visited by Jewish people. It is my impression in the forties and fifties Jews didn't drink—not in Pittsburgh anyway.

In high school I remember drinking twice. Once I spent the evening violently throwing up while my buddy Kenny Bluestone held on to me, I guess so I wouldn't fall over. The other time I punched the school tough guy, George Ardolino, right in the mouth, as he casually strolled down the street. George kindly took note of my condition and smiled. That's what I call tough.

When I first arrived in New York, just out of my teens, I was often in the company of a group of professors I knew who could toss it back pretty good. At that point I wasn't touching the stuff, which definitely made everyone else self-conscious. A little later, at acting class parties, I would get hold of a bottle of Thunderbird wine. I think it cost eighty-nine cents, but it certainly did the trick. About twenty years went by when I don't think I drank at all. This all changed in 1976 in Hawaii, where I was on location making the movie *King Kong*. Over a period of about three weeks, along with some pals, I seemed to be attempting to make up for the previous twenty years of abstinence. It actually changed my life. I realized I was capable of having a wonderful time every night of my life. When I finished the picture, I was determined to continue having that wonderful time every night—but without the liquor. With it, it was obvious I might have a wonderful time every night of my life; it would just be a short life.

Things evened out over the years. I'll still have a drink here and there. The bottle of whiskey in the dining-room cabinet certainly wouldn't last fifteen years with me around now, but no liquor store owner would say I was particularly helping pay his bills.

My whole attitude on the subject now has to do with stress management. If you don't do yoga, meditation, or the twenty or so other things that are around which I don't—I'm not proud to say—an occasional drink here and there, now and then, can come in handy. I found the balance between relaxing and an upset stomach.

I must say one of the biggest jokes in our society is people high on alcohol telling people who reach out for drugs to just say no.

If we could have that kinder, gentler society with all it connotes, I think the alcohol and drug business would be all that would suffer. The problem is clearly not alcohol and drugs. The problem is stress.

Kindness can be the drink or drug for us all. Kindness and maybe an occasional glass of wine.

Grace is the absence of everything that indicates pain or difficulty, hesitation or incongruity.

—WILLIAM HAZLITT

Sexism

BEFORE I BEGAN TO write this piece, once again, as with "impotence," I had to check to see exactly what "sexism" meant. The dictionary says it has to do with discriminating in favor of one's sex or assuming a person's abilities or social functions are determined by his or her sex. What I have to say doesn't really have to do with that—I don't think.

My problem is how to show verbal affection to a woman I don't know well without being insulting. This has always been a problem for me because when I want to be particularly friendly, I will sometimes say what I have to say and then tack on a "honey" or a "dear." Most recently it came up when a young couple were being interviewed by the board of the co-op apartment building I live in in New York. I'm on the board but not on the committee that generally does these interviews. People go before a tribunal of three board members, where primarily their finances are discussed. Because of some scheduling problems, this young couple came up before the whole board. So I was there to watch what I considered to be a difficult and sometimes inappropriate interrogation. I sat there suffering silently for a while, and after the young woman struggled through an answer to a question I didn't think should have been asked, I blurted, "That's all right, honey." She turned and mouthed "Thanks" to me. The rest of the board in part I'm sure resented my amiability, and the woman's husband seemed to grow more tense. The minute the "honey" was out of my mouth I was sure I had made a gaffe far worse than the rough interrogation. When I got home, I told my wife the story. She showed no reaction at all but after a long silence said she didn't feel I should have hit the woman with a "honey."

How could I have communicated my caring? Even though I'm a professional actor, I'm not that confident I could have packed enough warmth into a "That's all right, Mrs. So-and-So." What's the trouble with "honey" anyway? The following week I was working with some people, and I looked at one of the women and asked her how she would feel about being referred to as "honey." She said she never minded being called anything that a man would be called. In other words, no "honey"s for her either.

I realize the problem has to do with sounding patronizing. I have always had good relationships with women, except, of course, in certain close relationships. Even in those cases I don't believe I have any female enemies in my life. I've always had a wonderful relationship with my mother and quite honestly have never intended to patronize any woman, or man for that matter.

I believe at times I could have justly been accused of being detached, preoccupied, displaying inappropriate humor, among other things I'd rather not mention—but never patronizing. If I were one of those old, kindly guys who play doctors or mailmen on television, I'm sure I could communicate enough warmth just by calling a person Mrs. So-and-So, but in my case I feel I need the "honey."

I have gone way out of my way not to be accused of being patronizing, sexist, practicing sexism, chauvinistic, or any of that stuff. At one time my six best friends were women. I have a high awareness on all of this, and yet one heartfelt "honey" slips out of me, and it's Hitler time.

Oddly enough, when any woman I know or don't know calls me "honey," I love it. Go figure.

No hero is mortal till he dies.

—W. H. AUDEN

Heroes

I'VE HAD TWO HEROES in my adult life—Ralph Nader and Cesar Chavez—and have been fortunate enough to know them both. To me a hero is someone who selflessly devotes his life to others, and of course, we've had millions of them—soldiers, policemen, firemen, scientists, etc. Ralph Nader and Cesar Chavez were people I could see and read about over a period of years, so they became my heroes I could follow.

I went to visit Cesar Chavez in 1969. He lived in an extremely modest house in Delano, California. I went to a union meeting where he presided. Most of the discussion was about whether they would have food or a band at an upcoming celebration. They couldn't afford both. Cesar told me that in the famous photograph where Robert Kennedy hands him a wafer to break one of his long fasts, that was the second time Mr. Kennedy handed the wafer. The photographers missed it when he first handed it and asked for a retake.

When I spent an evening with Ralph Nader, he mostly wanted to talk about the best way to host *Saturday Night Live*, which we both had done—he a little better than I, I would say.

In childhood I had lots of heroes—Superman, Batman, but mostly the Lone Ranger. There was something about the way he would always ride off before anyone had a chance to thank him, and there'd always be one guy who'd say, "Who was that masked man?" I got a particular thrill when the answer would come, "Why, that was the Lone Ranger!"

Several years ago there was quite a to-do in the news about the Lone Ranger. Some Hollywood producers were planning a new movie about him and were searching around for someone to play him.

For all of our lives there has been only one Lone Ranger, and his name is Clayton Moore. We all grew up with him on television; even as we grew older, he was still there. But now Hollywood wanted to make a big movie out of the Lone Ranger, and Clayton Moore was seventy. Oh, he was still around. In fact, he was still around as the Lone Ranger. Nobody had seen him leap up on that many horses lately, but he was still showing up at parades and rodeos, and getting plenty of cheers and applause, too.

But Hollywood was making a new, big Lone Ranger movie, and the search was on for the new, young Lone Ranger. The producers of the movie felt it would not be in their interest to have two Lone Rangers around, so they went to court to get a ruling to force Clayton Moore to take off his mask and stop showing up as the Lone Ranger. And they won. Our Lone Ranger was ordered to take off his mask.

Well, Clayton Moore had worn this mask his whole life. Without it, well, he just wasn't the Lone Ranger. And if you've been the Lone Ranger your whole life, it's kind of tough, at seventy, to take off your mask and stop being him. So Clayton Moore went to court and protested the ruling. But he lost. He had to take off his mask.

Years earlier there was a headline in a New York newspaper that stayed with me; it read: SUPERMAN

COMMITS SUICIDE. George Reeves, who had been Superman as long as Clayton Moore had been the Lone Ranger, had committed suicide after he became despondent over being unable to find work as an actor after the *Superman* television series was canceled. Whenever he would try to get a part in something, they would say: "We can't use you in that part. People will say, 'That's Superman!'" And so he couldn't get a job, got very depressed, and ended his own life.

Clayton Moore was fighting back. When the court ordered him to take off his mask, he appealed the decision to a higher court. And the next time anyone saw him in public, he had taken off the mask pending appeal. But in its place was a very large pair of dark sunglasses. Not a bad mask in its own right. He showed up with those big dark sunglasses that covered just as much of his face as the mask had, and the applause and cheers were bigger than ever. The public was on his side.

Meanwhile, the Hollywood producers found a young man named Klinton Spilsbury, and he was the new Lone Ranger. The movie was made, it came out, and nobody went to see it. There were at least a couple of reasons for this: It hadn't gotten good reviews, and also, by the time it came out, there was quite a lot of public resentment over taking the mask off our Lone Ranger.

Eventually a higher court ruled that Clayton Moore could wear the mask after all. The glasses came off, the mask went back on, and Clayton Moore was getting bigger cheers than ever before.

Shortly after this I was at a party and I got into a conversation with a young actor who turned out to be Klinton Spilsbury, the new movie's Lone Ranger. He told me that he was a very serious actor from New York, had studied quite a lot, and was really doing very well moving up the ladder when this Lone Ranger opportunity came along. He said the movie was a mess, there were several scripts, and no one could agree on whether they were supposed to be funny or serious. When I asked him who the producer was, he absolutely couldn't remember his name; he considered it a good sign that he was finally able to totally block it from his mind. It had not been a happy experience. He was having difficulty in finding work because of his association with the movie and had moved back to New York to try to pick up the pieces of his career. The movie had a devastating effect on everyone except Clayton Moore, who was more popular than ever.

When I was a kid, we had a saying: "Don't mess with the Lone Ranger."

I feel somewhat like the boy in Kentucky who stubbed his toe while running to see his sweetheart. The boy said he was too big to cry, and far too badly hurt to laugh.

—ABRAHAM LINCOLN

Getting Fired

I'VE BEEN FIRED A number of times. The first time I was working as a car jockey for a Buick dealership in Pittsburgh. I was seventeen. My job was to move these new Buicks around in a big car warehouse. My problem was I had never driven a car that moved forward just by putting it in drive. A number of new Buicks didn't look so new after I had been there a few days. The boss called me over on a Wednesday and said he wouldn't be needing me on Thursday. I said, "So I should come in on Friday?" He said, "Not then either." Since I had never been fired, I didn't understand. "So I'll see you next week?" "No, we won't be needing you then either." I slowly got the message. It was a good lesson in cause and effect.

The next time I was fired I had a part-time job selling women's shoes in Miami, Florida, where I was going to college. I was an intensely preoccupied eighteen-year-old. I had a lot of things on my mind, and shoes weren't one of them. After not being able to find two or three shoes that customers had worn into the store, the manager called me over and said my performance was below shoe store standards. We shook hands, and I left before I put him out of business.

Next came my show business firings. The first time I was nineteen. At this point I was averaging one a year.

Someone got the idea to give me a song to sing in a musical we were doing in summer stock. I still can't imagine why. After a couple of days someone else was singing my song.

My last firing, so far, came about fifteen years later. It was an Off-Broadway play. The original lead was fired, then replaced by another man, who was fired. Then they asked me to go in. I knew what had happened to the first two actors, but I was unemployed, so I went in. The show started to be received better, and the producer felt since the show was now better, they should get a star to play my part in order to help get them out of the red, which all these firings had put them into. The playwright's son said, "Gee, Dad, I wouldn't fire this Grodin guy. I'd keep *him.*" The director, who was a famous actor, took over after they fired me; the show opened, got insufficient reviews to run, and closed. They said the star was miscast. Since the director-star was also a close friend of mine (I had actually recommended him for the directing job), this one ended a job and a friendship. This was the only time I disagreed with my firing.

A year later Neil Simon wrote a movie based on a story this same playwright had written, and much to the playwright's shock I was cast in the leading role. That was *The Heartbreak Kid*. Also, I wrote a play about someone getting fired that became a success.

I've always tried to learn from getting fired. I never spent much time on anger or resentment. I try to see where the firers are coming from. In the case of the play, the last one, the producer who fired me was coming from drugs.

Maybe the Great God of Firing thought I had some injustice coming to me for all those lost shoes, banged-up Buicks, and lousy singing.

I just read this piece over and realized I forgot two

more times I was fired. Both were when I was working for *Candid Camera* about five years before my last firing. I think I forgot because just about everybody who worked for *Candid Camera* was fired. It was like part of the job. My final firing there came when Allen Funt asked me to put a door that wouldn't open on a men's room at JFK airport. I argued against the idea basically because people heading to a men's room after a flight aren't ideal candidates for a practical joke. Mr. Funt insisted, and when we told these frustrated people they were on *Candid Camera,* their reactions were not amusing. Of course, it never made the air, and I was fired. Allen somehow blamed it all on me.

It's good to remember almost everyone gets fired in his lifetime. You are not alone. These firings can actually end up being funny stories you can tell—after several years.

Anger makes dull men witty, but it keeps them poor.

—ELIZABETH I

Unconscious Hostility

I THINK YOU CAN measure the degree of your unconscious hostility by the amount of times you find yourself saying, "I'm only kidding." It's something I've had to get on top of over the years, and a lot of people who work in comedy never do or care to.

I never wanted to take part in celebrity roasts. It always seemed to me to be a socially acceptable way to hurt someone publicly and get laughs at the same time. Recently I expressed that opinion to a man who's famous for his brilliance at roasts. He confided he felt the same way.

In the movie *Awakenings*, a board member says to Robert De Niro, "Are you aware of your unconscious hostility?" He responds, "If it's unconscious, how can I be aware of it?" Of course, that's the problem. All of us have unconscious hostility, and it can easily come out at people for whom you have no hostility at all. Hostile people, which we all are to a degree, just have it floating out there, and if you come into contact with them at the wrong moment, it will float out on you or, more accurately, stun you. It's hard at those moments to believe that it has nothing to do with you because it sure feels like it does.

Hostile humor is a tough one to get on top of. Along with "just kidding," you'll hear "I meant that as a joke" a lot. The real test we can apply here is: Is the other person laughing? If all these so-called jokes fall flat more often than not, check yourself. Personally I don't do put-down humor socially anymore. You just never know when it hits that wrong chord.

Years ago I was seated next to a very wealthy woman at a dinner party. She was a major investor in movies and Broadway shows, and she listed for me all the projects she had invested in. They had an impressive array of stars, directors, etc. After she finished, she looked to me for comment. I should have said something like "Well, that sure looks good. I wish you well." Instead, I said, "Well, it all looks good on paper." It must have really jolted her, because I heard about it the next day from my host. It was said that I was dishing out some pretty good servings of inappropriate humor. It's not that easy when you deal in humor so consistently professionally and personally to always be absolutely sure when you're being appropriate.

In the case of the woman investor, I probably had a built-in resistance to this recitation of where all her millions were going. She was an heiress, so she probably just allocated the money. I had tried to raise money for theatrical ventures over the years, and sometimes it feels like it would be easier to walk on your hands to Philadelphia. That's probably where my "it all looks good on paper" remark really came from. Now I do a lot of "That's great," "I wish you well" to people who hold forth.

Personally I never speak much of lofty aspirations or successes. I don't believe people in the same industry sit around rooting for each other. I had an actor friend years ago who had been around about ten years longer than I had. When I started to work and have my picture in the paper, etc., I made a point of never mentioning it to him as we watched basketball games together. Eventually he spotted me in the papers and brought it up. I kind of shrugged it off, but he became increasingly caustic the more successful I became. After a while it got so bad I chose to watch the basketball games by myself.

Unconscious hostility is a big deal. If it didn't exist, "Dear Abby" might not publish so often.

Everybody is ignorant, only on different subjects.

—WILL ROGERS

What You Don't Know
Won't Hurt You

I WAS SITTING AT dinner with a couple who were friends of mine, and the woman began to talk about how difficult she found it to walk down the street in New York City. She said the streets were so crowded that she was constantly being jostled, and by the time she reached the end of her day she was exhausted from all the jostling and the ducking and dodging of more jostling. She said she had finally solved the problem by always picking out a large man who was walking in the direction she was and getting into step behind him, letting him unknowingly lead the way.

I told her that I found her story particularly interesting because it just went to show you how many different kinds of problems people could have. I said that I had never had any real problems walking down the street in New York but that I had problems that they probably didn't have. Her husband, a particularly neurotic man (he'd already sent his food back to the restaurant's kitchen three times that night), found that really hard to believe.

I said one of my problems was with blankets.

"What about blankets?" my neurotic friend asked.

I said, "Well, when you stay in a hotel, do you assume that they've changed the blankets in your room before you check in?"

The man's mouth dropped open. "They don't?" he exclaimed.

"They certainly don't," I said.

"I never thought of that!" he said, suddenly deep in thought.

His wife said, "I have, and that's why I'm always careful to turn the sheet over the blanket. What gets me," she went on, "is the bedspreads. Those filthy bedspreads that have been over those blankets that haven't been changed in who knows how long."

The man, seeming to go slightly into shock, said, "I've never thought of any of this!"

I went on, saying, "I mean, who knows who was in those rooms over the weeks, even possibly months, before you got there, and who knows what they might have done on those blankets?"

"Or bedspreads," the woman added.

The man, growing paler by the minute, said, "I absolutely never thought of any of this!"

I said, "I always call ahead to the hotel and specifically ask them, as nicely as I can, if they would be sure that there would be fresh blankets on the bed."

"That's a good idea," the man said.

I said, "I mean, I ask for extra hangers and sometimes a board under the mattress first, but the call is really about those fresh blankets."

"What about the bedspread?" the woman asked.

"Well," I said, "lately I've been asking for a fresh bedspread, too. But I figure the part of the bedspread that touches the blanket is, of course, the inside part, and it's fairly unlikely anything too much has happened on the inside part of the bedspread, so I'm not as insistent on the bedspread."

The woman nodded uneasily. The man said again, "I've never thought of any of this!"

"I don't particularly like making these calls," I told them, "so whenever possible, I try to get someone else to do it for me."

"Who?" the man asked quickly.

"Well, when I flew out to Los Angeles to be on *The Tonight Show* recently, I asked the agency that represents me to do it. When I've done it in the past, the hotels are always pretty nice about it, although sometimes you can sense a slight edge there. But no hotel has ever claimed that those blankets are automatically changed."

"I'm amazed," the man said.

"In fact," I said, "the only time that something really unusual has happened was on this recent trip out for *The Tonight Show*." The couple leaned forward.

"The agency had called and arranged for the hangers, the board, and the blankets, and I checked into a very nice room at the Beverly Hills Hotel. After I had unpacked my suitcase, using all the extra hangers in the closet, the phone rang. It was the assistant manager of the hotel wanting to know if everything was satisfactory."

"That was nice," the woman said.

I nodded, "He then asked me, in a voice unmistakably tinged with sarcasm, if the blankets met with my approval."

"He didn't!" the man said.

"He did," I said. "I was instantly offended by his tone and quickly said, in a voice considerably friendlier than his, that I hadn't had a chance to check the blankets yet, but I was sure that everything was fine. 'How are the sheets?' he asked, in a voice with even more sarcasm than the earlier blanket question. I was now really getting angry, but I kept on in a polite manner, saying, 'Well, I'm sure the sheets are just fine.' Then I said, 'Have I offended you in some way?'"

"Good for you," my male friend said.

"The assistant manager replied that this was the Beverly Hills Hotel, and he never had received such a request in all his years there. I said I didn't mean to offend him or his hotel, but my experience told me that no hotel automatically changes its blankets for each new guest, no matter how much it charges you."

"Did you say that?" my male friend asked.

"I certainly did," I said.

"Good for you!" the couple chimed in.

"The assistant manager said he, in fact, was offended by my request and hoped everything was satisfactory to my taste. I assured him it was, in as friendly a tone as I could muster, and we said good-bye.

"Within a minute after I put the phone down, I was furious at the rudeness of the call. I'd flown out to Los Angeles to be on *The Tonight Show* with Johnny Carson, and this was the last thing I needed to happen. Being on *The Tonight Show* is not exactly the easiest thing in the world to do, and one of the reasons I had asked my agency to make all those blanket arrangements was just to avoid any unnecessary edginess on the day of the show. I was just about to call the assistant manager back to tell him what I thought of him when the phone rang again. It was my agent in the lobby. I was running late now for our lunch date, so I told him I'd be right down.

"As we were driving to the restaurant, I told the agent the whole story, how upset I was and how I really didn't need something like that on the day of *The Tonight Show*. The agent, a pixyish man in his sixties named Joe Schoenfeld, who at that time was the co-head of the movie department at the William Morris Agency, just had a bemused smile on his face as I told him the story. When I finished, he looked at me and said, 'Are you seriously telling me you didn't know that was me on the phone?' I looked at him, shocked and relieved at the same time. This was the same Joe Schoenfeld, it was coming back to me now, who had once called a prominent American film director at three in the morning in some country in Europe where he was with the director, saying he was calling from immigration, and told the man he'd better get over to immigration headquarters right away. The man almost had a heart attack rushing over there, to be greeted by Joe, who was in hysterics."

"What an agent!" my male friend exclaimed.

"Anyway, after I realized it was Joe, I kind of relaxed. Now all I had to worry about was *The Tonight Show.*" I said, "Before I found out it was Joe, I was starting to wonder what that assistant manager might have done to the blankets that were on the bed. That's why, by the way, I'm always very reluctant to send food back in a restaurant as you have. You never know what an angry chef could conceal in what's coming back to you."

My male friend grew pale once more. "My God," he said, "I've never thought of that either!"

Not guilty—but don't do it again.

Give Yourself a Break

WE'VE ALL MET PEOPLE who treat others badly and don't seem to notice the hurt they've caused. They go on their merry way building a list of people who hate them. Maybe someday someone tells them off, and they always look completely shocked. Then for a little while they may be careful, but within a few days they're back to their hurtful, bullying ways.

Then there are people who seem to feel guilty about a whole lot of things at the drop of a hat. Sometimes maybe they've done the wrong thing. Often it's hard to follow exactly what they feel so bad about. I used to be one of those people. I had things bothering me that would take a half hour to explain, and at the end of it some pretty smart people still wouldn't know what I was talking about. In my case I believe this all started when I lost my father. I was eighteen. He was fifty-three. For years, like millions of people who lose someone close, I felt responsibility. At one point it was so bad someone could point out a beautiful view and I wouldn't look because I felt I didn't deserve to see it. It took about twenty years for me to grow out of this and start to give myself a break.

Today I thankfully still have a high awareness of trying to do the right thing, but if I inadvertently offend and am made aware of it, I say I'm sorry and move on. I don't spend a lot of time beating myself up. Sometimes if my favorite sports team loses, I get in a frame of mind that I can suddenly remember bad stuff I did as a teenager that I wouldn't even admit to here. I know there must be a moral as well as legal statute of limitations, but still, I'm not talking. My only way out of that is to remember to give myself a break.

I have friends, not only Catholics, who feel terrible about a thought or feeling. One came late to dinner and dropped to his knees and begged forgiveness. He was only partially kidding. The world may be filled with hostile, evil people, but most of us aren't.

It sometimes feels like so much of life is spent in conflict with other people and ourselves. I find that by giving myself a break, I give it to others, too.

[Re not doing housework] After the first four years, the dirt doesn't get any worse.

—QUENTIN CRISP

Washing Your Food

WHEN I WAS A BOY growing up in Pittsburgh, my mother used to wash most of our food before cooking it. I'm not exactly sure why she did this, but I was raised in an Orthodox Jewish home, so that may have had something to do with it.

I was surprised, as I got out into the world, that I was looked at somewhat askance as I picked up this washing tradition. People would say to me, "What are you washing that piece of meat for? Anything questionable on it won't be there after it's boiled or baked or broiled. You're washing away important juices," they'd say. But it was too late. There was absolutely nothing I could do about it. That family washing tradition had gone too deep for me to change.

But even though I was a committed washer of food, I wasn't ready for what I ran into when I went to Marrakesh, in Morocco, to make a movie. I had my good friend Richard Martini there working with me. Among Martini's many talents is his ability to make friends instantly. I had sent him out one day to buy two rugs I had seen. Marrakesh is the rug capital of the world, and you pay a fraction there of what you would pay for these beauties elsewhere. The merchants there are also energetic negotiators. It's all considered par for the course, and I was told that anything less than a hot and heavy negotiation was

357

downright insulting. I've never had much of an appetite for this, so I sent Martini, who seems to be able to rise to any occasion. In this case, in the middle of the negotiations, rather than rising, he fell . . . down to his knees and then flat out on the rug, screaming, "Pleeeeeze, don't charge me so much money." The rug seller was startled and just stared at Martini, who now reduced his plea to one long, extended, high-pitched word: "Pleeeeeeeeeeeze!" After a couple of moments the seller was amused and started to laugh at Martini, which is just what he wanted, of course. The merchant then got right down there on the floor, and the two of them, lying there, tried to out-"Pleeeeeeeeze" each other. Richard ended up buying the rug at a pretty good price. The rug merchant was now one of Richard's best friends and insisted on accompanying him to the other rug seller who had the second rug I asked Richard to buy. Here both Martini and the first rug merchant threw themselves at the feet of the second rug seller early in the negotiations, and both shouted out, "Pleeeeeeeeze." The second rug seller, a stern, heavyset man, was not even mildly amused. Eventually, though, an acceptable deal was made after Richard stood up.

As the first rug seller was helping Richard into a taxi with the two rugs, he was so sorry to see his newfound friend go out of his life that he invited him to his apartment for dinner that night. Richard said he had made plans with me, and the rug seller said he'd be delighted to have both of us. Richard said he'd call him after he checked with me.

Richard came back to the hotel and told me the whole story. On coming over to Morocco, we'd been advised not to go strolling out on our own and particularly to be very, very careful of what we ate. In fact, the list of shots we were advised to take in America before leaving were enough to give anyone pause about going. I had taken some of the shots; Richard had taken none. He had mixed feelings about accepting the dinner invitation and, knowing me to be a lot more cautious than he, was shocked when I said I'd like to go. I figured how often do I get a chance to see how local Moroccans live. Richard called, saying we were coming, and the rug merchant, Abdullah, said he would have a few friends over and serve a special dish.

That night Abdullah and a friend picked us up in a car and took us to his apartment. It wasn't that different from a lot of New York apartments I'd seen and lived in, including cockroaches.

There were five Moroccan men there and the woman friend of one of them. They spoke very, very little English, and I, of course, spoke no Arabic, so we weren't exactly trading subtle anecdotes. At one point Richard left with Abdullah to pick up some special bread, and I was left alone with the group. They grinned at me, and I grinned back. Searching for a possible common interest to attempt to converse on, I asked, "What's for dinner?" The spokesman explained they were going to serve a dish called tagine. I asked what tagine was. It was explained to me, who grasped about one out of every twenty of his words, that tagine was lamb with herbs and lemon. I smiled, nodded, and said, "That sounds great."

He then added, amidst many words: "We prepare it all together, then take a shower with it."

My smile faded. I said I didn't quite understand. He repeated that once they got dinner together, they took a shower with it. "Oh, God," I thought, "this is what all those shots were about!" I still couldn't quite accept what he'd said, so I stood up and, pantomiming taking a shower, said: "This is what we mean when we say 'shower,'" trusting that they would laugh over the misunderstanding. But they only nodded and said, "Yes, shower." My mind was racing. I, of course, knew people stepped on grapes with their feet to make wine, so in a sense, I guess it wasn't that big a jump to take a shower with your dinner. Not a big jump, but certainly not one I wanted to make.

Accepting they planned to take dinner into the shower shortly and trying to buy time, I pressed on, asking them why. After about ten minutes of me trying to glean an English word out of masses of Arabic, I finally, with great effort, understood that in each apartment building there was a man in the basement who shoveled coal on the fire to give hot water for, among other things, the shower. This same man maintained large stoves, onto which the tagine was put, in crocks, to cook for hours. It seems the only word in that explanation that came out clearly in English was "shower"; therefore, the misunderstanding. Dinner would be forthcoming from a large crock and not someone's tub.

Even an old food washer like me wouldn't have been ready for that one.

It used to be a good hotel, but that proves nothing—I used to be a good boy.

—MARK TWAIN

Other People's Places
(Landlords and Hotels)

IT'S BEEN REPORTED THAT Eugene O'Neill's last words were "Born in a hotel room and, goddammit, died in a hotel room." Spending an entire adult life in show business does put you into a lot of hotel rooms, or apartments, or houses—other people's places.

Happily the worst of these came when I was very young. I had just arrived in New York, barely out of my teens. The excitement of beginning a career was so great that I barely noticed that I lived in a single room in a squalid hotel. It was dark in the middle of the sunniest day because my one window looked out on a narrow air shaft. It was on the fourth floor, Room 410, too far from the roof for any light to filter down. What did come down around three every afternoon were empty bottles thrown from above, usually accompanied by shouts of "son of a bitch" at best. The bathroom was down the hall, shared by easily fifteen people. It was the worst place I ever lived, but at twenty I didn't mind. It was "my place."

Oddly enough, the closest thing to that place I stayed in was a motel in Globe, Arizona, some thirty years later. Here I had two of these rooms. There was a window that looked out at a massive copper slag heap across the road. Behind the motel about thirty feet away was the railroad track, which I hadn't seen. Luckily the first time the train went by, it was the middle of the afternoon. The place shook so violently you'd have to think earthquake, but from the bathroom window I saw the train. If that train had first come by in the middle of the night . . . forget it. This, too, however, was a wonderful place because in the next room were my wife and newborn son. We were all there because I was on the road making the movie *Midnight Run*. The place is not always the thing.

Conversely, other places the movies have taken me have been grand and luxurious, and I have had less good times. I was living on the side of a mountain in a house on stilts in Los Angeles when an earthquake really did hit. Someone later told me houses on stilts are the safest during earthquakes—someone *later* told me.

I once lived in a gorgeous house on top of Mulholland Drive with a view whose only limit was the distance you could see. My wife and I moved in Saturday night. Sunday morning we went out to get some supplies. When we came home, a large rat came skittering across the wooden floor toward us. Sunday afternoon we checked into a very expensive hotel. There the bellhop looked at me as though I were nuts to mind that you couldn't lock your door from within. "The only people who have keys to the suites besides yourself are hotel staff," he said reassuringly. I used the phrase, "There's a flaw in your system," about five times before someone installed a chain latch.

I stayed at a beautiful inn in New Zealand which provided a van for transportation to town. I made a normal move to get in and cracked my head so hard I almost passed out. Later I mentioned to someone at the desk that maybe the van's roof was weird and people should be cautioned. The guy very nicely said, "Oh, that happens every day here."

I once rented a house in Los Angeles where the previous tenant had been evicted for reasons I never knew. About 2:00 A.M. the first night I was there he used his key and opened the front door. Fortunately, being the kind of person I am, I had a latch installed that afternoon—stopping his entry. I went to the door in the darkness. He was standing there with another man. He wanted me to come outside, so he could show me his lease, which he claimed gave *him* the right to be there, not me. I said we'd deal with it in the morning. About a year later I was renting another house, and this man moved in next door. Pretty soon there was a procession of people day and night, arriving at his house in limos, in pickup trucks—everything and every type of person imaginable. It turned out he was a famous abortionist.

I rented another house in Los Angeles that I was going through with a pal of mine. My wife was going to arrive the next day. Suddenly my friend stopped in a hallway, stared at a painting, and said, "Whoa! What's that!" After close examination we realized it was erotic art. After a lot of turning sideways, standing far away and close, we realized the house was *filled* with erotic or pornographic art.

I rented a house in Connecticut for years where the owners didn't see anything wrong with coming in and looking around when I wasn't there. There was nothing there I could have been arrested for or even make an *Enquirer* story, but . . . well, y'know.

On balance, when I look back at all the rentals, I think of a song Billie Holiday used to sing. "Mama may have, Papa may have, but God bless the child that has its own."

Television: A medium, so called, because it is neither rare nor well done.

—Ernie Kovacs

Cooperating with the Media

I WAS SITTING IN my apartment one afternoon looking out the window when I got a phone call from someone I didn't know asking me if I could help him out with a problem. This fellow had just arrived in New York from Los Angeles with a television crew for a cable program in order to do an interview with the sex symbol Morgan Fairchild. It seemed that Morgan was suddenly ill, and here was an expensive crew standing around with no one to interview. The guy was asking if I would possibly do him a favor and come right down to the Off-Broadway theater where Morgan was appearing in a play to do the interview in her absence. He said he and the crew had to leave right away to go back to Los Angeles because of all the expense of being in New York, and if they returned empty-handed, he could get fired.

About a half an hour later, when I arrived at the theater, the interviewer thankfully greeted me, introduced me to the crew, and quickly ushered me into a side room to discuss the interview. As soon as we were alone, he took out a pad and pen and asked me what movies I'd been in. I stared at him for a moment, and he apologized that he hadn't done any research on me, having, naturally, spent all his time preparing for Morgan Fairchild. I told him I understood the situation, but I frankly felt a little uncomfortable listing off all my show business credits. Maybe the biggest advantage or relief I experienced in getting to a point of being recognized was that I didn't any longer have to go through life reciting a résumé, and while I certainly understood the dilemma of the interviewer, I still wasn't all that happy to recite my list. He had a very short amount of time in the theater, so I offered a solution: Since he already had prepared a list of questions for Morgan Fairchild, why didn't he just ask me Morgan's questions, and who would know the difference? He liked the idea. Here is the part of the interview that stays in my mind:

"Do you think you're as sexy as Loni Anderson?"

"In my own way, yes."

"Did you believe in petting as a teenager?"

"I certainly did."

"Did you have sex in high school?"

"Sex?"

"Do you ever get real moody around a certain time of the month?"

"Not really."

"How important is it for you to show off your body and the way you dress?"

"Not that important."

"Do you ever get uncomfortable with the way men look at you?"

"Sometimes."

"If you have sex with someone, would you speak about it?"

"Not during."

"Do you ever feel you're being asked to show too much cleavage?"

"No."

"Is there any particular man you'd love to play a torrid love scene with?"

"No."

If you have had enough of your friend, lend him some money.

—RUSSIAN PROVERB

Loaning Money

SOMEONE ONCE SAID, "No good deed goes unpunished." In the case of loaning money, that has been my experience more than once. I lost a very close friend because I loaned him a good amount of money over the years. He has been unable to pay me back and assumes I'm angry with him for this, even though I've told him I'm not. I never counted on getting the money back. I believe the truth is he's angry with himself. I'm only sorry he's had a bad time. Even though I've lent a lot of money to people, I would never have done it if I couldn't afford to lose it.

There's another fellow, a former friend, who called to borrow some money. When I said, OK, he upped the figure. When I said OK again, he upped the figure again. Then I said, "What's going on?" I sent him the second figure, not the third, and have never heard from him since. He's never returned my calls, which have been to see how he's doing, not to ask for money.

I offered to loan money to another friend who was in difficulty, but he refused it, saying, "I can't see how I could ever pay you back." So I gave it to him and said it's a gift. He cried.

I have been repaid about 5 percent of all the money I've loaned in my life. I don't consider myself unusually generous because to a degree this has been my charity.

I've always been wary of formal charities since I know that some of them take a startling high percentage of what they receive for "administrative costs." I think millions of people would benefit if a verified agency would vouch for just what goes where. I'm sure such a body exists now, but it's not widely enough known.

I was once asked to appear for a charity on television, and the people told me I would announce large corporate contributions as though they had just come in when in fact, they were already pledged. These bulletin announcements were supposed to provoke more giving from the general public. I declined to appear.

I believe a lot of us would reach deeper if we *knew* what we gave would get to the needy.

Do not do unto others as you would they should do unto you. Their tastes may not be the same.

—GEORGE BERNARD SHAW

Manners/Etiquette

THIS WHOLE SUBJECT MAKES me edgy. I'm not even all that crazy about its existence. I'd rather people just be nice and let it go at that. Instead, we have all this stuff with which knives and forks, left and right, who gets introduced to whom first. All that nonsense.

Personally I've been eating at people's homes and restaurants for years, and all I really can retain is the smaller fork is for the salad—I think. I couldn't set a table to save my life. I just have no idea what goes left or right probably because I never cared. The whole subject strikes me as odd as people who easily walk by homeless people lying on the sidewalk to get to a movie theater and then are bitterly offended by the language in the movie.

Like everyone, I've eaten desserts with forks and been told I should be using a spoon and, of course, vice versa. I regularly am the last one to remember to put my napkin on my lap. Don't misunderstand me, I always get it there—I'm just often the last one. Sometimes the waiter does it for me with a fake smile.

I mean, what is the point of all this? I'm not for going back to caveman-style cuisine, but there must be something between that and jackets with ties and rules.

Actually I once *did* go to a Moroccan restaurant and everyone dug in with their hands. I was with Simon and Garfunkel and Ringo Starr. It was still disgusting.

379

Of course, in England in prior centuries it was even more complicated—calling cards and much more of when to do what with this and that and who knows! I suspect that people who seriously get into all of this are a little light of involvement with the rest of life. Otherwise how could they possibly have the time and focus?

I'm sure during wars and national disasters this extreme etiquette stuff really takes a back backseat, where it belongs.

However, while I think the subject of etiquette can be overdone, I do believe strongly in phone manners. I won't make a phone call that requires more than a moment without first asking the other person, "Did I get you in the middle of something?" or "Is this a good time to talk?" or "What were you just doing?" Actually the last question might not be a good one, but I sure don't want to launch right in with someone who's not ready for launch.

While at first look this may sound like I'm being sensitive, the truth is I don't want to be embarrassed. Five minutes into my point I don't want someone to suddenly say, "Look, can I call you back? I'm having sex." Actually I did call someone once whom I didn't ask if he was in the middle of something. The person spoke a few minutes in a rushed way and then asked if he could call me back tomorrow. When he did, he apologized for being short, but he *was* having sex when I called.

It's not that I'm afraid of causing coitus interruptus (to explain why a person takes a phone call during sex would be a book in itself—one I sure couldn't write), but I think it's likely when you call someone he's often not staring into space, and even staring into space is not something I'm secure enough to interrupt.

One of the problems with all of this is some people don't care if they're interrupted at any time, like when they're eating. I don't know if these eater-talkers would mind listening to someone chew in their ears, but I do. And it's hard to get off the phone with them too.

Me

Look, I've got you in the middle of lunch. Let me call you back.

Eater

Chew, chew, no, that's OK. I don't mind, chew, chew, chew.

Me

No, really, that's OK. I can call you later.

Eater

Chew, no, chew, what's, chew, going on? Chew.

Frankly one of my purposes of writing this is to inhibit these phone eaters. I've never been able to bring myself to say to an otherwise perfectly nice person who's eating a tuna in my ear, "Hey, are you nuts? Would you go to a restaurant and chew in someone's ear? What's the matter with you, you insensitive idiot?" Hence a chapter.

Aside from getting someone in the middle of something, I think it's a good idea to take the emotional temperature of the other person. You don't want to go on and on about an unpleasant exchange at work to someone who just lost a parent or even someone who already *has* a headache.

I also try to get off the phone before the other person says he has to. When I've failed at that, I'm left to wonder how many minutes have I embarrassed myself. So I get off quickly. Too quickly I'm told, as I've sometimes left people wondering what they've said to cause me to suddenly bail out.

My one everlasting regret on the subject comes from that moment as I'm putting the phone down and the other person calls out something I can't really hear. Often it sounds like "I love you" (wishful thinking?), but I've missed it. I've never been able to call back and ask if she just said she loved me. Chances are they didn't but are sitting there angry because it feels like I've hung up on them.

Funny how you can start out with the intention of being the most sensitive, careful person in the world and end up hurting a lot of people's feelings.

I guess extremes of any kind are questionable.

Nothing in the world can take the place of persistence.

Talent will not; nothing is more common than unsuccessful men with talent.

Genius will not; unrewarded genius is almost a proverb.

Education will not; the world is full of educated derelicts.

Persistence and determination alone are omnipotent.

— CALVIN COOLIDGE

The Power of Spite

I ONCE DIRECTED A play in New York where a critic said in the first line of his review that the playwright had stolen two hours out of his life. In this critic's case he probably meant he had to put his glass down at the bar for two hours in order to see the play. Meanness in that review and others made me determined to give this play a chance to run. (I was also one of its producers.) By using all methods known to man and some yet unknown at that time, we managed to make the play the longest-running play on Broadway that season. I did it out of spite. If the play wasn't sufficiently entertaining in spite of what some critics said, it couldn't have run. The facts speak for themselves. It was.

I think I owe a lot of my career to spite. If I had not been so attacked and ridiculed as a young actor in school, I wonder if I would have tried as hard. Probably, but still, I wonder. There's something about the certainty of people's abuse that fuels my fire. It doesn't seem to matter that for centuries so-called experts have been proven wrong over and over again. Nothing slows these abusers down.

I think some of us are like fighters who truly come to life when they take their biggest blow. So to all of you who take delight in attacking, you may be empowering the very people you would like to see go away.

It seems like fitting justice.

On Boston: Clear out eight hundred thousand people and preserve it as a museum piece.

—FRANK LLOYD WRIGHT

Museums

I'VE NEVER LIVED UP to expectations of me regarding museums. People perceive me as a guy who probably spends several hours a week in museums. I don't.

It's not that I dislike museums. In fact, I really do like the Museum of Natural History a lot. It's got big dinosaur skeletons and mostly incredible nature scenes—a lot of little and big stuffed animals doing their thing in their natural environment. The problem is the Museum of Natural History exhausts me. Of course, it exhausts me when I go with my four-year-old because *any* place I go with my four-year-old that has open space—look out! But it exhausts me when I go with anyone because everyone I know seems ready to see the whole damn thing as long as they're there, and this place is enormous. I mean, like five floors. At some point I can get them to check out the cafeteria, but even there it's such a mob scene—forget it.

Like most places, my way of going to a museum is check it out for a while and then go someplace else—like home. The exception is if there's something funny going on; then I stay anywhere till it's closed. I tried to *get* something funny to go on on one trip to the Natural History. They had a special exhibit of great sports legends. It seemed odd when I saw the sign. I couldn't figure out what that had to do with its usual stuff. After looking at

stuffed squirrels and muskrats and bears and lions for a
while, I wandered over and asked a young woman who
worked there if they had any stuffed sports legends in
the exhibit. She naturally stared at me. I said the animals
were all stuffed. "Do you have Babe Ruth or someone
like that stuffed back there?" After a long moment when
she determined, I hope, I wasn't insane, she said they
had videotapes and plaques but no one stuffed. I said,
"Y'know, Roy Rogers had his horse Trigger stuffed, and
he's standing out there grazing in the pasture." That's
really true, but the young woman just reiterated, "No,
no stuffed sports legends."

The other big museum in New York that I'm more or
less regularly dragged to is the internationally acclaimed
Metropolitan Museum of Art. I mean, this place is huge
and filled with treasure. Masterpieces of paintings. Glori-
ous sculpture. Jewelry from all ages. It's incredible, and
I'm still only good for about twenty minutes. Believe me,
I realize some people who like me may despise me after
that admission, but I'm not looking for love here, only
truth. I can't really explain why I only have twenty for
the museum. It's like it's out of my realm or something.
I know they're geniuses who painted and sculpted, etc.;
it's just not my thing. My thing is a guy making a diving
catch for a touchdown. Something like that.

My most troublesome experience at the Metropolitan
came when my wife took me there to show me this room
that Frank Lloyd Wright designed. It was the talk of the
place. I came in, checked it out, and, I'm embarrassed to
say, threw something this side of a tantrum. I mean, every place for two people to sit down faced a wall. If you
had four people visiting in this room, each couple would
be looking at different walls. There were no little areas
arranged, so a small group could sit and talk. I remember
Frank Lloyd Wright as an austere man who had his

places grow out of the mountains and things—definitely not a fella who seemed like he wanted some group chatting—but hey! Give me a break! Personally I'd get lonely pretty fast if I had to sit facing a wall all day. I mean, the wall was *close!* Even if someone was sitting next to me, staring at that wall wouldn't do either one of us any good. The whole thing had an element of punishment about it.

When I left the museum that day, I apologized to my wife as I know I overreacted. The whole experience probably touched off something in my childhood: being made to go somewhere you didn't want to go and then having to like it, too—like school. The open space of the room, and there was plenty of it, with all the chairs along the sides facing the wall, could make a pretty good indoor touch football field, but I wisely kept that observation to myself.

The good news is that no one tries very hard to get me to go there anymore. Don't misunderstand me, I realize I'm wrong about all this. I know I should try to develop these absent cultural tastes of mine, and I'm sure I could, if life expectancy were doubled.

"That's bigamy."

"Yes, and it's big of me, too. It's big of all of us. I'm sick of these conventional marriages. One woman and one man was good enough for your grandmother. But who wants to marry your grandmother?"

—GROUCHO MARX

I BELIEVE MARRIAGES SUCCEED or fail based on expectations.

When people get married, they've pretty much seen the best of each other and not that much of the worst. Otherwise why would they get married?

However, people can show their best for only a limited amount of time. Eventually the truth comes out.

A couple who are friends of mine were thinking of getting a divorce. I asked the man what the problem was. The problems he had with his wife I never even thought of. He wanted his child bathed and fed by the time he got home from work. His wife couldn't seem to get that to happen with sufficient consistency. I said I wouldn't dream of asking that of my wife. As anyone who has ever taken care of a child, especially a two-to-four-year-old boy, knows it's the hardest job in the world. Recently, as an experiment, a professional football player followed a three-year-old boy around for a day. After a couple of hours the player had to take a nap.

My friend also objected that his wife would, only on occasion, accompany him to various functions. I would never ask my wife to go anywhere she doesn't want. This isn't because I'm such a great guy. It's because I want the same treatment.

Also, unless I'm coming home from working a fourteen-hour day, I don't mind being responsible for getting

395

my own dinner. Under normal circumstances I have more time than my wife, who is the primary caretaker of our four-year-old boy. Primary caretakers of four-year-olds, like the football player, must use all spare time to nap.

So what do I expect from marriage? Faithfulness would be first. I prefer not to be yelled at by my wife, especially in public. A sense of caring how I'm doing from time to time is nice, but maybe most important, a sense of love not necessarily expressed but understood. Expressed actually makes me uneasy. Years ago I had a girl friend who liked to say, "You're my honey, and you always will be." I can't even write here, decades later, how badly that all ended.

So cook your own meals, do your own laundry and every other chore in the world, and consider yourself lucky if you've got loyalty, caring, and unexpressed love.

A Closing Note

SEVERAL YEARS AGO I had a friend, an eighty-eight-year-old man. I asked him what he felt was the most important thing he had learned in his life. He only thought for a moment, then simply said, "Take it easy." That was it. "Take it easy."

I took it to mean that from his vantage point he could see that he had invested too much emotion in too many things that really didn't matter. It seemed like a good piece of advice fifteen years ago, and today I can't think of any better.

Nobody's perfect, especially me and you, so let's not sweat the small stuff. Sometimes when I watch *The Love Connection* on TV and see how men and women get agitated over their date's sport jacket or hair length or choice of restaurants, etc., I can see why there aren't a tremendous number of happy marriages or relationships of any kind.

Let the little things go. We have in common that we're on this planet for a relatively short time. If we can't love each other, then let's at least give each other a break. Everyone is having a harder time than it appears.